Assessment: Study and succeed
in theory and practice

Other Quay titles by the same authors

Management in the Acute Ward

Assessment of Clinical Practice: The why, who, when and how of assessing nursing practice

Assessment: Study and succeed in theory and practice

Jane Walton and Maggie Reeves

Quay
Books

Mark Allen
Publishing Ltd

Quay Books Division, Mark Allen Publishing Limited
Jesses Farm, Snow Hill, Dinton, Wiltshire, SP3 5HN

British Library Cataloguing-in-Publication Data
A catalogue record is available for this book

© Mark Allen Publishing Ltd 2001
ISBN 1 85642 183 X

Printed in the UK by The Cromwell Press, Trowbridge, Wiltshire

Contents

Foreword

This book is a valuable addition to the material available to students who wish to have a greater understanding of the assessment process. Professional courses at all academic levels are continuing to develop their assessment strategies for the collation of knowledge, skills and attitudes. Assessors of both theory and practice continue to develop methodologies for this process in an ever changing profession.

Students entering a professional course must find the process of assessment in both theory and practice daunting. The continuing and varied nature of this process with deadlines to meet and outcomes to achieve is a challenge not to be taken lightly. The authors of this book have approached this subject in a logical user-friendly manner. I particularly like the way in which the text outlines the students' responsibility while clearly identifying the help and support available. The progression of the text through the different types of assessment to tips on how to get the best from assessment is a pleasure to read. All students will identify with the characters used to demonstrate learning styles and the problems they bring to individuals; the suggestion for peer support and group learning should enable students to explore this particular learning strategy.

The methodology used to introduce students to the work of other authors on the process of assessment in the final pages of the book is interesting. I particularly like the way in which the authors have chosen to give a brief resumé of the context of other authors' work, this gives students the opportunity to select other texts on learning material without having to undertake extensive research or reading.

The planning and implementation process for assessment advocated by this book provides an excellent working tool, the authors should be congratulated.

Hilary Walker
Education office
July, 2000

Acknowledgements

The idea for writing this book has come from the authors' years of working with students. We would like to thank those students for the 'trials and tribulations' involved in assisting them, where possible to successful completion of their courses. It has been a valuable and beneficial learning experience for us both. We would also like to thank friends and colleagues who have assisted and supported us in our work.

Our especial thanks go to Hilary Walker for her continued encouragement and support in the writing of this book, and for writing the *Foreword*.

We would also to like to acknowledge the help and support we have received from David Walton and Mike Reeves. We promise that this is our last book.

Jane would especially like to express her thanks to Maggie. Her hard work and support has made this book possible and thanks also for being a good colleague, nurse and friend.

Introduction

The aim of this book is to give the responsibility of your studies to you, the student, fair and square.

Please do not stop reading at this point because you:

1. Think you have just wasted your money buying this book.
2. Thought you had bought a book that would do the studying and make life easier for you; not give you responsibilities.

With most difficult things in life it is worth remembering that there are people on the sidelines whose job it is to help you meet your full potential. This book is designed to help you to help yourself, but with the help of others around you.

This book looks at ways and means of studying to achieve success. Success in university/theory-led assessment and also in assessment of practice in vocational courses. The success will be yours to enjoy due to your work.

The proverb that 'you reap what you sow' is very pertinent for the work you do on the course you are on. Like so many things in life, the more you put into something the more you will get out of it.

The style of each section is different. For example,

Chapter 1	Asks you a series of questions about 'assessment'.
Chapter 2	Gives an overview of various types of assessment, both theory and practice and states their benefits to you.
Chapter 3	Looks at who is on your side when theoretical assessment comes your way.
Chapter 4	Tackles how to make the most of practice-based assessment.
Chapter 5	Looks at how to benefit from peer and self-assessment.
Chapter 6	Contains the serious side of the book. It reviews a selection of study skills type books available at the moment. It is not an exhaustive review but may save you some hard work when hunting through books.
Chapter 7	Summarises a variety of tips to help you use and 'beat the system'.

Throughout the book four student friends feature and do a review of its contents. They are using the material as they study on different courses around the country. They keep tabs on each other and encourage each other to succeed. These friends are as different from each other as could be possible. We bring in examples related to the strengths and weaknesses identified.

Bertie Brilliance has always stunned his friends with his academic ability. He masters new concepts without turning a hair, but has his failings in the practical areas of life. He can be a bit boring and overbearing and has been at university the longest. He is studying physiotherapy.

Bertie.Brilliance@cerebral.ac.uk

He is complemented by **Practical Prunella** who likes 'doing' things and has recently triumphed at long last by gaining a place on a nursing course. She is intelligent but finds communicating on paper much harder than demonstrating ability in action.

Prunella@practicalfreeserve.co.uk

Her best friend is **Frantic Philomena**. She is dreadfully disorganised in her approach to life and try as she might is always doing things at the last minute, when she has to sacrifice quality for quantity to achieve time scales. Her studies are in occupational therapy.

Frantic.Philomena@internetrush.uk

Their fourth friend is **Charlie Average-Lazy**. He happily lopes through life without putting much effort into anything. He always manages to 'get by' with everything he does. He has a winning smile which works wonders on elderly aunts and gullible grannies. He uses it to the full (but not very often successfully) when he wishes to extract a favour from tutorial or clinical staff. He is studying to be a radiographer.

CharlieAvLazy@medullamansions.net

Do you recognise yourself in any of these characters? If not, you might as you read this book.

We hope you enjoy working through this book and that your efforts bring you the rewards you deserve.

There is no intended reference here to a particular course and its students. Any one of these four students can be found on any course.

1
Thoughts on assessment

What's the point of learning if you are not made aware of your level of learning? As painful as it may be, assessment has this function of making you aware of your learning achievements.

Remember there will always be more learning, 'you are never too old to learn', or 'learning never stops'. So assessment will never be complete. It will not only make you aware of your learning but also illustrate areas of further learning/development for you. So, let's enjoy it.

Different people prefer different types of assessment and it is impossible to please everyone. For example, theoretical assessment is not Prunella's favourite and practical assessment eludes Bertie. Students react differently when it comes to applying themselves to the requirements of the various assessment schemes of the courses studied. It leads to the possible starting point of assessment.

A positive view of assessment and its challenge is a great help

A positive view of assessment from a student's internal perspective can be referred to as intrinsic motivation. It is said you learn more purposefully if you are intrinsically motivated.

Have you ever questioned: Why should I have to be assessed? Why should I have to do the work involved?

This is often Charlie's question, as he would much rather be out clubbing.

Any assessment should start with you – you need to take a look at yourself

Let's consider where you stand with regard to assessment:

- what do you like about assessment — make a list
- what do you dislike about assessment — make a list.

Believe it or not some people do like to be assessed.

By comparing and contrasting the two lists you often find there are similar aspects in both, for example 'It makes me work'. Imagine a course without assessment – a course where you will only be given a certificate of attendance. Would this mean that you would work? Would you feel that you had actually achieved anything?

Your strengths and weaknesses related to studying/learning/ assessment

Think about the following:

- what are your strengths and weaknesses regarding, a) learning and b) assessment?
- what motivates you?
- how are you going to cope with yourself and with others during this course?
- how are others going to cope with you?

Identifying some of these factors can help you decide on the right approach to study and allow you to seek help in the most beneficial way for your individual needs.

Times of study and assessment can be very fraught especially when time, and particularly quiet time, is required. You can help yourself with this by recognising when you work best. Are you a morning, evening or night person? Others can help you if they recognise the time when you work best and keep quiet.

None of the students being discussed in this book have stated family responsibilities and/or dependants. Charlie's attitude might be different if he was recently married or Philomena might be more organised if she had children to organise as well as herself.

Strengths and weaknesses

You may find that you like to work alone or that you like to work with others in a small group. Think about setting up your study connections. If you find that you are rather worried about the fact of being watched in practical work, or producing written work, setting up a study group may help you find confidence in the knowledge that you have on a subject either practice- or theory-based. Also others in the group may discuss their anxieties allowing you to realise that you are not alone in your worries. Remember a worry shared is a worry halved.

What motivates you to work, to achieve

It would appear that Charlie does not have much motivation as he just lollops along in life. Learning can be defined as a change in behaviour, which is either permanent or semi-permanent. That change in behaviour has to occur in you, not in anyone else. You have to make an effort to make that change. For Charlie to succeed on his course he needs to change his approach. The assessments he does should help to make him work, to make him change, to allow him to develop rather than just keep smiling his way through life. The same could happen to you.

Coping with yourself and others

Studying can create conflicts for you. Your already tight schedule has to accommodate extra time to read and take in new information without falling asleep over the books or without your mind drifting over the multitude of things that you need to get done before tomorrow. Tension can run high creating many other frictions. Philomena is very good at this.

Plans of action are advised both for your personal life and your study life. One important piece of advice – do not neglect your social life but put it in perspective and let your relatives/friends know. Relatives/friends can be sympathetic and at times very helpful.

How are others going to cope with you?

In fact, some people like to help. A friend/relative helping you by looking after the children, giving you lifts, doing practical things like the shopping, will feel that they have also acquired an award.

Do not go underground with your studies as relatives/friends may not be the same when you surface.

Benefits of assessment

Setting a level/standard

You can feel very pleased and proud of yourself when you achieve the level/standard. You should also feel safe and confident that you are performing correctly and that your knowledge and understanding is accurate. This refers both to the assessment of theory and practice. In healthcare it is essential that you know you are doing the best for the patient/client.

Letting you know about yourself and others know about you

Assessment results can inform you of your learning and also let others know not only your achievements but also your difficulties. This can allow you not only to recognise your strengths but also your weaknesses or, in other words, the areas where you need to improve. It can also mean that others may see where you need extra help, such as Philomena needing help with organising herself.

Remember, we are all going to be different in the way that we learn and what we are able to learn and master. It can also mean that others may recognise your talents and direct you forward in a more meaningful, individualised way. For example, results of general education assessment have possibly led you in selecting the career that links to your academic strengths.

Assessment can help you in other ways

It has selected you specially

You have been selected through a process of assessment to start a course. Whatever qualifications or previous experience were needed on application you have now achieved them. So, be confident. It is possible for you to be successful on your course.

It has allowed you to undertake a course: it has opened the course to you

The course is not open to anyone and everyone.

The course with its assessment structure can give you the opening to the job/position/career that you want. Throughout the course you will have the opportunity to get the help and advice that you need to be successful, so take advantage of it. The attitude you take towards your course will usually be reflected in the results.

The outcome of the course is not going to be open to everyone

Consider, just as the initial entry was not open to everyone so the eventual outcome/qualification of the course is not available to all. This is a sad fact of life so determine that you are going to be one of the successful ones.

Bertie may think that he is going to be successful as theoretical/ academic work comes easily to him but he should learn not to be too complacent as practical work will require some effort from him.

New message:

Prunella@practicalfreeserve.co.uk
Frantic.Philomena@internetrush.uk
CharlieAvLazy@medullamansions.net

I think I've found the book which will help all of us. You've got to get your own copy so you can work through it! I wish it had been available when I started my course.

Bertie

2
Overview of various types of assessment

This chapter is divided into two parts:

Part 1:   **Useful background knowledge**
          Assessment related to theory
          Assessment related to practice

Part II: **Various methods of assessment**
          Assessment of theory
          Assessment of practice

Part I: Useful background knowledge

There are many and ingenious ways that have been designed to test the theory and practice component of any subject you may decide to study. The following section will look at some of the different assessment types and their purpose. Hopefully this will enable you to organise your study and construct your work in the most advantageous manner. Bertie may relish this section whereas Charlie will avoid it – getting by on the minimum – but this does not mean getting the best out of his studies.

Some students prefer one type of assessment to another, but normally there is no choice. For example, because Prunella is good at practical skills she prefers demonstrating these rather than doing theoretical work. With every type of assessment there will be instructions. Many students of our acquaintance get into a panic when they hear about being assessed and then forget to concentrate on what they have got to do. It might be interesting for you to observe how often the panic of the situation gets in the way of your peers taking in the required information. Questions which have just been answered will be asked again and again.

Most courses have a range of assessment methods, including: essays, demonstrations, project work, examinations, journals, practicals, presentations, portfolios and profiles.

In this range you will find that there are some you like more than others.

Before looking at these methods in detail it is important to set the scene on two other relevant aspects of the assessment process which are present in most assessment schemes. These are formative and summative work, and the taxonomy of educational objectives.

Formative and summative work appears in both theoretical and practical assessments. Formative work is often not formally assessed, that is given a mark or grade, but its importance is to show the student and tutor how well the student is progressing. Any advice given should be listened to carefully. For example, the tutor may say of your essay outline, 'this is on the right lines, but I suggest you expand on these two points'. This does **not** mean that your work will receive a pass grade unless you respond correctly to the suggestion. Such assessment will give you an indication as to how much work has to be done and the areas for concentrated study. It is like a 'mock' or 'practice'. Always write down comments from tutorials (formative assessment), it might help you to remember what to do.

The **real thing** is the summative part of the assessment, from which the mark for progress or classification on the course is derived. Formative assessment should have prepared you for the actual assessment work, if you use the guidance and support you have been offered.

Assessment related to theory

Theoretical achievement can be measured in objectives.

Taxonomy of educational objectives

Within theoretical assessment Bloom (1956) devised what is called a 'Taxonomy of educational objectives'. This is a classification of progression in the 'cognitive domain', and is often linked to marking criteria. Hopefully things will become clearer as this paragraph progresses. There are six layers or levels which are built on top of each other in a pyramid (see *Figure 2.1*). Each of the layers is required within the ones above it. When a student has reached the top of the pyramid in a certain subject they can be considered to have reached a high cognitive level.

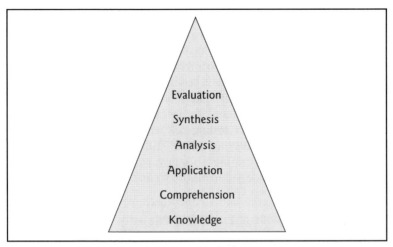

Figure 2.1: Taxonomy of educational objectives

Quinn (1995) gives a good commentary on the taxonomy. The following is a paraphrase from his chapter on curriculum planning.

A more detailed breakdown of the components of educational objectives is found on page12, *Figure 2.2* where each of the levels is subdivided for greater clarification.

The following is our breakdown of the objectives with examples:

Knowledge is fundamental to all the layers. It can be tested by recall of facts, trends, terminology, criteria and theories. The verbs which can be used to introduce the assessment of knowledge are define, describe, identify, label, name, state, and list.

* For example, name the capital of New Zealand, or name a theory which relates to your practice.

Comprehension takes knowledge further. Interpret or translate are two verbs which can be used when testing understanding of a subject. Other verbs could be: paraphrase, convert, explain and give examples.

* For example, read the section (in a prescribed text) on what constitutes a capital city, and summarise it in your own words. Or, give examples where the theory mentioned above can be used in practice and explain in your own words a theory which relates to your practice.

Application is particularly important in courses of study with a vocational focus. Rules, principles and concepts have to be used in different contexts. Prunella, for example, needs to have knowledge of the drugs which are being administered. She also has to know that drugs can have different names according to the drug companies that make the product. This has to be applied in the practical arena when selecting the bottle that contains the relevant drug.

Verbs used for the testing of application could include: demonstrate, relate, use, solve and show. Although drug administration is a simple example, there are so many ways whereby theoretical knowledge has to be understood before it can be applied in practice.

* For example, using the knowledge you have gained about 'what constitutes a capital city', and using London as an example, outline which of these features apply. Or, relate the theory identified under 'knowledge' to your practical experience.

Analysis is where information is broken down into component parts which can also be prioritised. A specimen, which is sent for analysis, gets all sorts of treatment such as slicing, viewing from all angles and being tested against something. This is what the student has to do with the information under analysis. You need to look at the information from all angles.

* For example, a site may be X-rayed from several different angles. A case conference may analyse a patient's situation from the viewpoints of a doctor, nurse, physiotherapist, occupational therapist or radiographer. Academically or in theory, analysis means using work from other authors as well. Hence the need for references which, apart from anything else, mean that the reader can read the original him/herself.

Very often a student is asked to critically analyse a specific subject. This is looking at the subject more intensely, but not just for things that are wrong – good points as well as weak points need to be considered. Edwards (1998) gives some useful pointers for critical thinking and analysis in written assignments.

Verbs used by teachers to determine analysis include: discuss, differentiate, discriminate and distinguish.

* For example, discuss how devolution has affected the 'capital' status of Edinburgh. Or, discriminate between the component parts of the practice undertaken

You can often help each other as a group when doing analysis. Why not tape yourselves, or get someone to take detailed notes, as you discuss the issues involved. Take the different viewpoints expressed and find the relevant literature.

Synthesis is where the student mixes information to form another whole (like a synthesiser does with music). This process shows some creativity because the mix is likely to be different when undertaken by different students. Verbs used in assessment of synthesis include: compile, compose, create, devise and plan.

* For example, invent your ideal capital city – some computer games allow you to do this. Or, create a new alternative to the theory first presented. (If you take aspects from other theories and create a new one it is called 'eclectic'.)

Evaluation is the final level and is where a judgement is made about information and its value. This is measured against standards or criteria. Compare and contrast, criticise, justify, appraise and judge are typical assessment verbs. This could be, taking what you have synthesised a stage further, looking at the success/failure of the new product.

* For example, using the city you have invented, justify the suitability of the taxes you have imposed on the inhabitants for the 'capital city paraphernalia' you have had to build. Or, you have introduced a change in practice. Determine the effectiveness of the change.

The theoretical work, which you submit, will be assessed against criteria for the appropriate level. It is always wise to look at the 'marking criteria' and if you don't understand it, ask for an explanation. This is one way of ensuring that the work you submit is written appropriately. It is also a way of saving a great deal of time.

The grid in *Figure 2.2*, shows examples of the different educational objectives mentioned earlier and some of the descriptions of what should be included in your work to attain those objective. It also includes a section on the organisation of your work as that goes a long way towards your success. This grid will need to be read alongside your university's marking criteria and will help you to predict your grade (see *Figure 2.2*, overleaf).

Organisation Levels 1/2/3	Knowledge Levels 1/2/3	Comprehension Levels 1/2/3	Application Levels 1/2/3	Analysis Levels 2/3	Synthesis Levels 2/3	Evaluation Levels 2/4/3
Structure is clear and logical with good definition of topic. Referencing is appropriate and accurate. The work is well presented with excellent use of English.	Material presented is accurate and relevant from a wide variety of sources. The key issues are prominently addressed.	Demonstrates clear understanding of the issues concerned. Relevant research is applied to the subject.	Uses reflection and relevant research findings to apply theory to own practice.	The arguments presented are well organised with effective use of empirical evidence.	Demonstrates ability to analyse own assumptions, values and ideas in a constructive argument.	The strengths and weaknesses of the argument presented are clearly identified.
Structure shows logical planning. Referencing is adequate and accurate. Presentation is good with few grammatical or spelling errors.	Evidence of wide reading. Content is accurate and all key issues are addressed.	Demonstrates understanding of the literature and associated research.	Uses reflection in demonstrating the link between theory and practice.	Presents a sound argument using a variety of sources.	Argues convincingly using relevant supporting literature and attempts to form a logical conclusion.	The conclusion is clearly expressed and some strengths and weaknesses are demonstrated.

Figure 2.2: Grid using educational objectives for assessment of theory, devised by M Hutton (1998)

The work displays logical structure. Referencing is limited but accurate. Presentation is neat and academic style acceptable.	Evidence of reading from a small number of sources. Most content is both valid and accurate. Key issues are raised.	Demonstrates understanding of key issues but may include some areas of confusion.	Demonstrates how theory is linked to own practice.	Some valid arguments are presented but may contain inconsistencies.	Own views and arguments are not clearly stated but an attempt to draw conclusions is made.	Conclusions are logical and an attempt is made to demonstrate strengths and weaknesses.
The work below this line would be a bare pass grade						
Structure is weak. Referencing is incomplete and inaccurate. Presentation and style lack finesse.	Limited evidence of reading. Some content is inaccurate or irrelevant. Not all key issues are discussed.	Interpretation of knowledge is not always clear.	Application to practice is limited.	Argument contains major flaws. There is little comparison of views.	Describes findings/ views of others but fails to draw conclusions from them.	Conclusions drawn are vague or unrealistic
The work below this line would be a fail grade						
Structure is unclear. Referencing is lacking/incorrect. Presentation is poor and style immature.	Evidence of reading is limited/inappropriate. Majority of content is inaccurate/ irrelevant. Key issues are omitted.	Fails to demonstrate the link between theory and practice where relevant.	Does not compare and contrast a variety of views. No logical argument is developed.	Does not attempt to identify strengths and weaknesses in support of any conclusions.	Lacks logical conclusion.	Does not attempt to identify strengths and weaknesses in support of any conclusions.

Figure 2.2: cont.

These levels of educational objectives are linked to the hierarchy of academic levels used in higher education today. These are levels associated with 'CATS' points (Credit Accumulation and Transfer Scheme).

Students go to university to 'read' a subject. There are ways by which you can present this information by means of referring to the literature on the subject and incorporating the educational objectives.

Level 1 Description, comprehension and application.

Level 2 Analysis and discussion.

Level 3 Higher analysis, synthesis and evaluative judgement based on knowledge and experience gained.

On most full-time courses each of these three levels will normally be of a year's duration. Successful completion of a course of study at Level 1 will lead to a certificate in higher education. At Level 2 a diploma in higher education, and Level 3 work can lead to a degree or a degree with honours. One course which is slightly different is that for nurses undertaking a diploma in higher education, this may take three years with the clinical practice. Most universities now award CATS points for each level (see *Figure 2.3*).

Level 1 work 120 CATS points = Certificate in Higher Education
+
Level 2 work 120 CATS points = Diploma in Higher Education
+
Level 3 work 120 CATS points = Degree with Honours

To gain the complete award, the total of 360 CATS points need to be acquired

Figure 2.3: CATS points

Most students on vocational courses are awarded a professional qualification as well as the academic qualification. However, if you are a student who received your professional qualifications before CATS was 'invented', you should not think that your professional qualification is of any less value. Having said this, some universities award retrospective credits at Level 1 for courses that were completed some time ago.

There is also the possibility of writing a reflective profile about the learning which has taken place. This writing is for accreditation of prior experiential learning (AP[E]L). The aim is for the work to be awarded academic credits at the relevant level. This will need to be done according to the specific university's rules and regulations.

New message:

Bertie.Brilliance@cerebral.ac.uk

This is hard work, but just what you'd like. I think I've worked out one of the levels of taxonomy — because I always like to check things out with previous students. I must be able to do something on the comprehension level. Not like you brain box, you've got the analysis bit sussed with all your reading. I'd better see how Pru's getting on as this section will blow her mind, you know how she likes to get things right. She'll be the one to ask about the practical application side though. Cheers, Charlie

PS. Assessment of practice seems easier – or is it?

Assessment related to practice

For vocational courses there will always be another angle to the education process. Academic work leads to an academic award such as a diploma in higher education, whereas the practice-led assessment results in a professional qualification such as a physiotherapist, occupational therapist, radiographer or nurse. These assessments are normally concurrent. As the academic knowledge and cognitive skills develop, so the practical knowledge and expertise is developed.

The principle of formative assessment followed by summative assessment still applies for practical assessment in all courses. With practice-led assessment when you get feedback at the formative point in the experience, listen hard and do what is suggested. Hopefully, this will lead to success and competence at the summative point. This is particularly important because in the practice environment lives could be at risk. Although a theoretical piece of work takes up a lot of time and energy it is not a matter of life and death or an individual's discomfort. Unsafe practice must be prevented at all costs.

The purpose of practice-led assessments is to turn you from a novice to being competent over a period of time and to make sure that you are safe to deal with your patients/clients. However, do bear in mind that you will achieve this competence in practice at different stages throughout the course.

For assessment of practice you are likely to have a list of learning outcomes or competencies to achieve by the end of a period of time. As your course progresses so the level at which you are assessed rises. This is done to maintain a standard; a level by which a professional body measures your capabilities and suitability to practice.

Understanding levels of achievement can help you progress. There are several different ways of measuring the development of practical skills. Bloom (1956, mentioned earlier in this chapter) produced a series of stages to develop a skill known as the 'psychomotor taxonomy' as did Steinaker and Bell (see Walton and Reeves, 1999). Benner (1984) also describes a series of stages related to learning which end in producing an 'expert'.

We have looked at the above theories and suggest the following interpretation.

A psychomotor taxonomy of five stages: seeing and copying; doing under instruction; doing with concentration; doing fluently while using complementary skills and doing intuitively.

Stages of a psychomotor taxonomy

Seeing and copying

When you watch someone performing a skill it can look very easy. If you try to copy this skill, it is not quite as easy as it looked. Perhaps you can remember only parts of what is required and your hands become very clumsy. For you to be safe to carry out this skill, particularly if a patient or client is involved, you will need to remember your limitations and do the following:

- watch someone doing a skill
- recognise that when you copy the skill, you may require further help. Therefore you may need to perform the skill away from patients/clients to start with, eg. in a skills laboratory setting

- after watching and practising, perform the skill in reality under close supervision. Remember that apart from performing the skill you must know the theory behind the practice, especially the safety aspects.

To maintain the safety of all concerned, ensure someone watches you practise before you perform a similar skill in a different context.

Doing under instruction

This can follow seeing and copying or come separately. This is where you learn how to perform a skill using a 'hands on' approach with step by step instructions. These can be verbal or written.

Bertie enjoys any discussion before such a session, but still has difficulty putting the two together. He has developed coping strategies which are not always helpful, eg. asking awkward questions at the wrong moment/talking loudly to cover his anxiety/being over-bearing and trying to intimidate the person teaching the skill. Simple acceptance of his weakness, by listening to guidance and following it, may be his solution.

Doing with concentration

You are now safe to do the skill under observation but you are still very slow and have to think very carefully about the order of your actions. Sometimes the ablest of students such as Prunella can be so slow as to incur the comment from the watcher, 'It's quicker to do it myself'. She, and you, will speed up with practice. Practise is important. Doing something once does not necessarily lead to competent practice. Practise and practise again in a variety of settings. Experience develops from this approach.

Doing fluently using complementary skills

The skill has been mastered. You do not have to think about each stage, it comes quite naturally. Because you are relaxed you can now communicate with the patient/client and you are not constantly thinking of your next move. You may be informing them of what is happening or distracting them with light conversation – with them, not at them. Beware of inflicting your social life on your patients/ clients Charlie.

Doing intuitively

You can now do the skill, talk to the patient/client and observe other relevant details such as his/her facial expressions: are they showing pain, worry, or relief?

It is when you have achieved this final stage of 'doing intuitively' in all the expected learning outcomes or competencies for your course, that you will be considered 'competent'. Once all the other aspects of theoretical, university-led work have been successfully completed as well, you will be eligible for your award, academically and professionally. This is what a 'vocational' course is all about.

This is a brief outline of how a psychomotor skills taxonomy can be used. After achieving competence you can then move onwards and upwards to become an 'expert' (Benner, 1984).

It must be remembered that 'practice' is about combining theory and practice. With each skill you perform, there should also be a theoretical basis. You are advised to question the theory of the practice which you perform, and be sure of the research evidence base that supports each facet of your practice.

Being assessed in practice

This can be done by competency statements, learning outcomes or assessment objectives. Whichever terminology is used there will be a statement which indicates what must be achieved. The following discussion will refer to the intended outcomes of learning as 'competency statements', although learning outcomes or assessment objectives can also be terms used.

Competence is what you need to attain to qualify for your chosen career. Competence can be defined as ability, an area in which a person is competent, a skill, but in each of the chosen careers there is a variety of skills.

Some courses have competency statements indicating what you are to achieve, also many of these statements can be found in the Code of Conduct or Ethical Code of your profession.

One of the problems of competency statements is that they are broad, generalised statements that are open to a variety of inter-pretations. These varying interpretations might cause you some confusion but there are reasons for them being phrased as they are. It is worth understanding the reason to allow you to then utilise the statements.

Our four students have tried to get to grips with the competency statements related to their practice and have realised the following:

- their intended career is broad and varied
- each practical activity needs to accommodate the needs of the individual/s involved, although they recognise that there are common principles to aspects of care
- practical experiences of students cannot be absolutely identical
- different areas of practice offer differing experience
- students' levels of experience will influence what is expected of them.

Competencies are phrased to cover the overall intent but they need to be incorporated into your current area of practice.

The best way to understand competencies in practice is to break them down into the concrete terms stating the actual action you will need to complete. It must be recognised that when in practice you cannot encounter all aspects of care/treatment/skill. You should discuss what is achievable in a particular placement area according to your experience level.

When, for example, the words '**safe environment**' are incorporated into a competency statement it might be worded as, 'Ensure the safety of patients/clients and their visitors'.

Looking at this statement you might think, 'Well that is no problem I can do that!' But, what exactly does that mean?

In concrete/actual terms does it mean you must know:

- the fire procedure
- the cardiac arrest procedure and actually be able to perform it
- how to care for any patient/client requiring any treatment.

There could be a never ending series of questions. However, in each area of placement it is suggested that you find out exactly what is expected. Follow the stages below:

- take your assessment book/booklet with you to your area of placement

- consider your strengths and weaknesses and decide what you would like to develop in yourself during the placement
- make an appointment and see your mentor/supervisor
- discuss the statements in your practical documentation along with your own required developments
- agree a concrete plan of action.

For example, a plan of action concerning the competency of safety consists of:

* **Physiotherapy**: conduct an exercise class for six persons.

* **Radiography**: position four patients for their X-rays.

* **Occupational therapy:** conduct a home assessment for two patients.

* **Nurse**: carry out the care of a patient for a shift.

All of these activities can have the word safely written into them but they are actions that can be carried out in the practice area that could be used to meet the competency.

Message to:

Bertie.Brilliance@cerebral.ac.uk
CharlieAvLazy@medullamansions.net
Frantic.Philomena@internetrush.uk

This section on competencies, learning outcomes and objectives makes practical assessment more realistic. I can actually see that I can find out what I need to do to pass practical assessment now. I think it is important to understand about the theory I need as well. I am going to ask my assessor to watch me caring for a patient next week — a bit nerve wracking — but at least I hope she will tell me how I am doing and then I can ask questions especially about the theoretical application.

Prunella

Part 2: Various methods of assessment

Assessment of theory

Key points in the text will be highlighted. These points are also summarised in *Chapter 7*.

Essay writing

An essay is looking for written information in a prose format. There is normally a word limit to ensure you **refrain from 'waffle'** but also to see how you tackle a subject, prioritise points and summarise material. This is important. An essay, as with all other assessment methods, can test all six levels of Bloom's taxonomy discussed earlier. Most essays written for a university course will require that you use **evidence from other sources of literature** to justify a point you might be making if your essay is written at the level of 'application' and above. The essay does not usually ask for your personal comments.

Most study skills books (see *Chapter 6*) describe how an essay should be constructed. Do take note of these texts as the **structure of an essay** can make the difference between a pass and a fail grade. Make your essays 'marker friendly'– logical presentation allows for easier decisions. An essay which has a clear introduction, followed by the main body which tackles each point outlined in an orderly and 'flowing' manner will rate more highly than the essay that appears to be thrown together at the last minute by someone sitting in a moving train (a message for Philomena perhaps?). An additional bonus would be a good conclusion bringing together the key points of the essay and making a recommendation or summarising comment at the end.

One of the ways to ensure that an essay flows is to **plan it first**. This is such a simple solution to an insurmountable problem for some students. However you plan your essay, make sure you also put the items in order, so that one subject follows the previous one in a prioritised and logical fashion. Book a tutorial early so that you can check that your plan is on the right lines. Again, just the sort of arrangement Philomena ought to make.

Many universities have a word limit for pieces of work. **Do stick to the word limit**. 'Pruning' skills or 'padding' skills may need to be developed. This is a specific area in which you could ask for help. Make sure that you think about word limits as you plan, and perhaps pick fewer (or greater) points to work on in your essay.

Another, not quite so obvious tip is to **write the introduction at the end** of the essay writing process. Then you'll know what you have put in your essay and in which order. You can also state your intent in the introduction to match the sequence of the essay. You'll know how the definition you have selected will fit in (or not) and then you will also be able to write a sensible conclusion. When you have written your essay, get someone else (friend/longsuffering partner – usually not a tutor or a colleague on the course as they should know the assignment brief already) to read your work and tell you what the assignment wanted you to do. If the reader's answer is correct, your essay is on the right lines and is making sense.

Referencing your work

Many universities are taking the references involved in academic writing very seriously. Referencing, like any skill, takes practise. Make sure you acquire and **use the university's guide** to the preferred in-house style. For many students the referencing component of an essay is the hardest part, but it is also a technical area where marks can be accumulated by attention to detail. The whole process demands a disciplined approach and is an area of study that both Charlie and Philomena are going to have to work hard at. You can lose marks by doing silly things such as putting a reference in the text and not in the reference list, and vice versa.

Forgetting to **get the full reference when taking notes** is another aspect that with forethought, some paper and a pen you could easily avoid. Writing out the full quote as well as its source is more time-consuming in the short term but means you can add the reference to your assignment work quickly and easily without having to read the whole article/chapter again. You would be surprised at how much time you could save by these simple expedients. Always ask yourself, 'could I find this item again with the reference I have included?' If not, try again. This situation could cause last minute panic when the work needs to be handed in. It will not be considered as a suitable reason for an extension of assignment deadline. It is poor time management and lack of attention to detail.

Using the right language

There is a distinct difference between writing a postcard, writing a note to the milkman and writing an academic essay. Many students try to write a long postcard, or translate a conversation to paper and wonder why they don't get very high marks. One of the first things to do before writing is to read. Read professional journals, read academic text books (not the 'dry and dusty kind'), read to find out what others think, to get their style into your system. In most instances of academic writing you need to get away from the first person; I/me/my (plural we/our) and get to an impersonal or objective style. Sometimes it is appropriate to use the third person, ie. the student decided... or the author felt... Use your reading to help you.

This book is written in a more relaxed style than many text books. This has been done deliberately, so that you are not frightened off. A much more formal style has been adopted in *Chapter 6*. It illustrates the sort of impersonal or objective style you should aim at. You should be able to pick out the less formal bits.

Having said this, there are times when writing in the first person is the most appropriate style, for example, when writing your journal.

We have been looking at essay writing as a format for assessment. This can be used in various guises. A case or care study are types of essay, so is a project. Essays are also often required in an exam. These will now be explored.

Case/care study

This type of essay is one which is focused specifically on a patient or client (and their family), or on a specific area of practice.

Typically you are asked to select a patient or client or a situation within a family and discuss issues related to aspects of your clinical practice. For example, you may be asked to discuss the psychological, social and physiological aspects of a patient in your care. You could be asked about the way a family relates and reacts to an illness, or problem within a family. This work could be classed as a cross between an essay and a project in that there are specific sections that would have to be considered.

One of the interesting things about such a piece of work is that it can be an in-depth study about one patient or client, giving you the opportunity to look at an individual and what you have or could have done to improve the clinical situation. It is an apt way of linking theory with practice, and encourages you to look for research about different aspects of your practice to help you see how practice must be evidence-based. As with all essays you would need to reference your work.

In a completely different context, a case study approach could be used as a method of research.

Project work

A project is usually an assignment whereby different aspects of work have to be covered. You may be asked to investigate something that would require getting factual information from books and journals, as well as doing a placement visit to acquire first hand knowledge of a situation. Your project may be broken down into sections with specific requirements from each. Make sure you tackle each aspect, and don't miss a vital component. Your work may be of a high standard but be missing a vital part. **Don't fail on detail**. Within a project it is usually acceptable to put sub-headings to denote the pertinent parts of the work. This is also a way of keeping track of various components.

However you plan the project you will need to have an introduction, middle and conclusion as for any essay. A project is more likely to have an appendix than other essays. The normal convention is that an **appendix should not be longer than 10% of the whole essay**. Another aspect is that when you want your reader to look at the appendix, **tell them** to by saying, for example, 'see appendix A'. You would be surprised how many students expect the marker to practise telepathy.

Another aspect of a project is that it often requires the student to work in a group or team. This can be the best or worst of experiences, depending on the others. (Of course it would never be you that goes on holiday instead of doing the work /you that goes sick on the day of the presentation/you that leaves the vital poster on the bus or anything like that, would it?) But if Philomena or Charlie was in your presentation group, guess who would be doing all the work? Do try to get organised as soon as you know your working group. Swap names and addresses and other means of communication. **Set dates for meeting and goals for each session**. Try not to waste time talking about social activities at the expense of getting the work done, or spending your time moaning about having to do the work and calling the teacher lazy for this type of 'cop out' teaching (see

Chapter 3 for a useful list of tips on working in a team). From the teacher's perspective it is often more time-consuming than actually teaching the subject; but it is used as a valuable way for students to interact and learn for themselves. You learn best by doing. Group work is known as synergy – a way of learning from each other. It complements androgogy, the best way adults learn – by finding out for themselves. Even though this work is often formative, remember that it may save you a lot of work later when the summative work has to be done.

If you are lumbered with people in your group who do not pull their weight:

* First encourage them to participate. Bertie may need to be asked to help in a constructive manner rather than his, 'I know it all' approach. You might also need to set deadlines for Philomena. Charlie will need to be given specific responsibilities.

* Secondly, ask them if they want to swap groups (if that's possible) and get rid of them that way, especially if they are like Charlie and are not meeting the agreed commitments to the group.

* Alternatively, you could 'grass on' them to the tutorial staff. The way you could avoid the non-participants getting any credit for the work you've done is to ensure that a list of the workers goes on the work submitted, whether it is an essay type or a poster.

One of the hardest things to cope with in these circumstances is the group member who does not produce the work but still succeeds on the course, possibly with a better mark than you. This is one of life's ironies (see *Introduction*).

Examinations

The thought of exams can often cause people to react in some very peculiar ways. Prunella is great in a clinical setting but had a panic attack in an exam and had to leave the room. This may be a throw back from her school days, or a genuine fear of this type of 'unknown', and it affects many students.

For most courses exams are a necessary evil. One thing an exam does is to test the individual concerned. The problem with the multiplicity of assignments is that they can be reproduced very easily for another person and the whole arena of plagiarism is opened up. (By the way, most teachers **do** know the various ways in which you can/could cheat in various types of assignments. Reflect that the only person who is harmed is you. What a waste of effort.) Even though it is helpful to study in/with a group, **make sure you do your own work**, because on the exam day it will be you who is tested, so make sure you can show the markers you know the answers. This is one situation that Charlie can't smile his way through.

How can this rather unpopular form of assessment be made simpler? There are so many books written on the subject that it would be insulting to you to condense that help into a few brief lines. Some of the following tips may not appear in other texts.

Try to minimise the anxiety you feel about this type of assessment. It is important, but no more important than any other assignment essay. The only thing you have to do which is different is to remember facts and details, and to do this in a specified period of time. Get the 'system' to work for you by making sure that you have all the information that is available about the exam, the module, the topics and the expectations. This information helps you to get to grips with the reality of the situation and not the terror about the situation. Some students are short of the relevant handouts, instructions and details like date/time/venue.

Make sure you have this **basic** information for your examination campaign.

Questions you might ask about the different types of exams on the 'academic market'

* Is it a 'known topic(s)' exam? In other words, will you be told the areas of assessment? Make sure you know the topic(s). This type of exam helps you to focus on a section of the curriculum so that you can learn something in greater detail than the whole.

* What should I study? Most exams are of the 'unseen question' type. If appropriate, ask to see previous exam papers so that you can gauge how the questions are structured and what might be expected of you. Don't try to guess questions and make your studying too narrow – it's like predicting lottery numbers – it does not work. You could also ask for and **do practice questions** but make sure they are relevant questions. Find out if the tutor can look at these practice answers. This is often not possible for a variety of reasons. Why not swap your answers with your peer/ syndicate group instead. (You must be able to trust this group for obvious reasons.) Practice questions will allow you to marshal

your thoughts, enable you to practise planning the answer and help you to plan your time. A by-product might be wrist strengthening exercises. Many students have forgotten how to write for a sustained period of time due to long use of the word processor. Sitting down for two or three hours can also be torture for some, eg. if you have a health problem which makes it difficult to sit for long periods, report it to the relevant tutorial staff.

* Which questions should I choose? Choosing a question from a paper can be very difficult and time-consuming. Always make sure that you **read all the questions** carefully so that you understand what they are asking and not what you hope, or thought they were asking. This requires disciplined time management. Don't get tempted to write too quickly because others around you appear to be speed writing for a competition. Also, don't panic if on initial reading of the exam paper you can only see two out of five questions that you could tackle. Start with the question you like best but **don't spend too long on it** to the detriment of the less preferred questions. If this is one of your weaknesses, create a time plan alongside your answer plan.

Short answer papers are just that. If asked to outline/state/draw/fill in gaps; do just that. The marks awarded for each question will not change to accommodate a long answer so don't waste your time. These are quite useful exams because you can get marks in a relatively short period of time.

Another type of exam, which can be trickier, is that of multiple choice questions (MCQs). They are often subtitled 'multiple guess'. Find out how the questions will be marked. Sometimes negative marking is used, ie. if you get an answer wrong a mark is deducted. Such an MCQ paper can end up 'in the red' if more answers are wrong than right.You can't just rely on guesswork. Despite this, they are useful papers for factual information to be tested. Always **read the stem of the question and the four possible answers** before giving an answer. Unlike *Who Wants to Be a Millionaire?* you can't phone a friend, get a 50/50, or ask the audience.

Open book exams are yet another way of testing you in an examination environment. This type of exam can be used to test your comprehension of a topic area or to compare and contrast different texts. These exams sound good, especially to Charlie as he can read from the books used at the last minute. Prunella may need guidance as to which books might be helpful, while Bertie might think he knows it all so does not need books to help him in the exam.

The principle is that you are allowed to take a specified number of resources into the exam room. This can be a selection of books/ journals relevant to the topic area. You need to think about the material very carefully. Always take texts that are versatile and have key references in them. **Be selective** in the books you take in – know them fairly well. Many students spend so much time trying to find the quote they want that the time has gone and little is written.

If permitted, put 'Post-it'® notes on relevant pages so that you can find things quickly. Then, when you do your answer plan, number the sections and add these numbers to the sticky notes so that you can find the right quote immediately. **Don't let you exam desk become swamped with clutter**.

To move away from the exam format, there are yet more devious ways to test a student's knowledge, skills and attitudes.

Research critique

Most courses have a section on research. There are different aspects of research that can be tested. A common approach that is useful for students to gain a grasp of research that has been published is a 'critique'. A piece of research is selected and read and then it is critically analysed using other literature about the research process. This is a means of determining whether you can apply the research process to someone else's work and whether or not the researcher has kept to the 'rules' of research. It also helps you to conduct a literature search which is a process you need to learn, so that a subsequent literature review, a research proposal and/or dissertation can be written.

A research proposal is another way of testing a student's knowledge of research. You have to plan a piece of research which may, or may not, be carried out. In other words, you go through each stage of the research process and apply it to your study. The final way of testing research knowledge at a higher level is that of a 'dissertation'. A piece of research is undertaken from start to finish and is written up. The length, depth and complexity of the dissertation is determined by the level at which it is being assessed. For example, the work for a BSc (Hons) and a Master's degree would be different in lots of ways, but particularly in the extent that Bloom's taxonomy of educational objectives is fulfilled to the evaluative stage.

> When completing this type of work always **select a topic**
> **which interests you** at the start and which will also be
> relevant to your practice. This may prevent you from becoming
> very fed up with the topic after a while as you will be working
> on it extensively. It can also give a meaning and a purpose to
> your work as it can be applied to your practice.

There are two more areas of assessment to be discussed which are more personalised in presentation.

Seminars and poster presentations are very useful ways of showing how much you know. Normally you would be given a subject area to prepare for your student colleagues. Do **follow the brief** given to you for the presentation as there is normally a time limit and you should allow for questions to be asked. The time limit is also an indication of the amount of work you should put in. This type of assessment is normally 'formative' but it can still be very nerve wracking. One thing we can tell you is that the work you have prepared for such a presentation is not easily forgotten.

Always **listen to the feedback** (formative assessment) given after such torture; there may be lots of things for you to learn from your peers and from the tutorial staff. Despite your anxiety, try to listen to the other presentations as well as your own. You will learn a great deal from your peers and you need to listen so that you can give them constructive feedback, see *Chapter 5*. It is possibly best to ask to give your presentation first, then you can enjoy the others. Prunella would love this approach whereas Philomena would not be ready. She will probably be thinking about her topic as she listens to the rest of the presentations. Unfortunately, this means her presentation is likely to be disjointed, disorganised and will leave the audience disgruntled.

Diary, reflective journal, portfolio, profile

The final means of assessment for discussion is that of a diary/reflective journal. This is becoming a very popular form of assessment (although often formative) as it enables you to express yourself in a different and personal way. Will Philomena ever get round to doing hers? Charlie will most probably think it's a joke — but they do have important applications. For example, these journals can be used as part of your professional portfolio, and elements of them can be extracted for more public consumption for a variety of purposes, ie. a profile.

A portfolio is a collection of evidence from your personal and professional life demonstrating your acquisition of knowledge, skills and attitudes, past, present and potential. (Like all the photos ever taken of you.) The profile is a specific part of this portfolio which you have selected to present to a particular audience for a particular purpose (like a selected photo album which has been suitably edited). (See Brown, 1995 for further details.)

The journals and/or profiles can be used when you want to apply for a job at the end of the course. You will need to seek specific guidance as to the format required for your profession. Once in work you may find keeping a journal useful towards 'IPR' or whatever it may be called where you work. (IPR stands for individual performance review and is a time for setting and reviewing your goals and progress, and setting new targets for the future.) So, what better than having a written record of what you have done.

Different professions have specific requirements for their members. For example, qualified nurses need to maintain a personal, professional profile under the auspices of PREP (Post Registration Education and Practice).

Another use of profiles is to demonstrate what you have learned. This can be for accreditation of prior achievement (APA) or accreditation of prior experiential learning (AP[E]L) and is therefore summative (see *page 15*). Many courses have the facility to gain access to or to be exempt from an aspect of a course because learning has previously taken place. This is often very specific to the institution and you will always need to follow the instructions of the relevant university/ college to undertake this process (see Hull and Redfern, 1996; Nganasurian,1999 listed under 'References and further reading', *p.91*).

Message to:

Bertie.Brilliance@cerebral.ac.uk

Warning: collecting portfolios of evidence can seriously damage your hoarding capacity. Do not move house without checking you have kept your portfolio intact, and the relevant items are accessible when required! Keep your course work, letters of success from your university and any other evidence which can show you have completed a particular module of study or you have enough academic credits at the right level (CATS) to access another course in the future. (NB. warn your partner of this hazard and ensure they understand the importance of **not spring cleaning without your permission!**)

Fwd this to:

Prunella@practicalfreeserve.co.uk

Frantic.Philomena@internetrush.uk

CharlieAvLazy@medullamansions.net

Although reflective writing is often formative, some nursing courses are using reflection on aspects of clinical practice as part of the combined summative theoretical and practical assessment.

A 'new' nursing course is being introduced for the new millennium requiring students to maintain a personal portfolio of evidence that will enable them to be assessed at different points throughout the course. If successful in achieving the required learning outcomes, there will be the possibility of 'stepping off and stepping on' at different points of the course. This portfolio will enable the student to take the evidence to an employer if a break from the course is required, or can facilitate transfer to another higher education institution.

The final product will demonstrate that the student has reached the required academic standard, diploma or degree, and a professional qualification of Registered Nurse (RN).

For Prunella this would mean that she could possibly step off at the end of year one and move nearer to the love of her life.

Assessment on a vocational course also requires assessment of practice. There are different ways a student on a vocational course can be assessed in practice. This may be a one-off test of ability which may or may not have been practised beforehand. Alternatively, you may be assessed on a continuous basis. These processes will be looked at in greater depth in *Chapter 4* (see also Walton and Reeves, 1999.)

While learning practical skills, one aspect of practice-led assessment that a student should be aware of is being given the wrong information in a clinical setting and what to do about it. This is not commonplace but can cause the student problems. No practitioner is perfect, but each individual should strive to improve and to be up-to-date with the latest methods of care/treatment. If you find you are being taught out-of-date material it is important that you say something. However, it's not what you say but the way that you say it. You may wish to consult with a member of the tutorial staff/practice link staff to give you some moral or more substantial support.

It is vital that you get the most out of any practical experience. Placements are often at a premium and should be treated with care. If for any reason you cannot attend, you must inform the placement so that time is not wasted waiting for you to arrive, or arrangements made that you cannot keep. These may seem very obvious courtesies to most of you reading this, but you'd be surprised at how many students cause others great inconvenience by their lack of thought.

On a much more positive note, placements can be great fun and a tremendous experience, and all under supervision giving you a certain amount of support so that you can learn your chosen profession safely and competently.

New Message to:

Bertie.Brilliance@cerebral.ac.uk
Frantic.Philomena@internetrush.uk
CharlieAvLazy@medullamansions.net.

Dear All, I've got a horrible feeling that we must know the authors of this book. Are you sure they are not writing under a false name? It's a bit frightening to read about yourself on nearly every page. Help!

Prunella

3

Theoretical/educational-led assessment – who's on your side?

Contrary to popular opinion, those who teach, assess and support you are on your side. The reason that they want you to pass is a genuine wish for you to succeed. It takes up more time to fail, so don't use the 'I can learn from my mistakes' excuse but make the attempt to get it right first time.

When you start a new course, life can be very daunting but also exciting. You will meet many new people and be exposed to all sorts of patterns of behaviour, belief systems and ways of being taught. Depending on where you have recently studied, you may be quite comfortable with the way your course is taught. If you haven't studied for a while, or have been used to a 'spoon-feeding' style of teaching, you may find university a rude awakening. You may also have been used to a small group of fellow students who you knew quite well, and so did not mind discussing issues in front of them.

You may now be plunged into a course that has a group of 350 students, all equally nervous and wanting to do well. Alternatively, your course may only have six students, but a small group has its own problems as well.

Coping in a group – large or small

Coping with large groups

In a large group you can do one of several things:

1. Attend every session, sit at the front, be able to ask questions and get as much as you can out of every session that you attend.
2. Attend every session, sit in the middle, duck when a question is asked, hear most of what is being said, but be distracted by the students who are talking throughout the session.
3. Attend most sessions, sit at the back, miss half of what is being said, get bored and so talk, read, or anything apart from pay

attention.You will not be able to hear the answers from other students and you will get less and less from every session you attend. This may lead to:

- non-attendance at sessions – the feeling that there are 'so many students, I won't get missed syndrome'
- subsequent failure as you have not received from, or participated in, sessions.

We know students who fit into all of these categories. Often the pattern is set when you start a course. The friends you make will have an enormous influence on you. This can obviously be good or bad. When you start your course be 'on your own side' and determine what it is that you want from the course. Do you want: a good laugh, make loads of friends, go to parties all week, learn and get a qualification or something else? Not all of these options are mutually exclusive. Pick wisely – it may save you a lot of grief later.

Teaching strategies are also moderately predictable and limited in large groups. Lectures with overhead transparencies, gapped handouts, 'buzz groups' and consequent feedback. The aspect of feedback which can be the most useful for you, is often dreaded. You may have to construct a poster, or even worse, give verbal feedback in front of everyone. From experience this can often be interminable and you can't hear what's being said, however useful.

If you are asked for a poster make sure that the writing is large and clear with key words. This will mean that others can see it and there will be fewer questions for clarification.

If you are asked to give verbal feedback of your group's discussion, speak clearly and as far as possible unselfconsciously. If there is a microphone, don't be shy – use it. Try not to read the answers as your voice is projected in the direction you are looking, ie. down at your feet and your colleagues will not be able to hear. It is at this point that the rest of the group gets embarrassed, then starts to shuffle and talk. Another tip: **stand up, speak up and shut up**.

Three further tips regarding coping with group work and subsequent feedback:

1. When asked to get into groups, do so as quickly and as 'un-sheep like' as possible.
2. Don't waste time on social chit-chat, but get on with the task in hand.
3. Decide quickly and at the beginning who is going to give the feedback so that your group does not look stupid for being disorganised. Take it in turns to give the feedback.

No one would ever suggest that really large groups are the ideal way of education, but they can serve a purpose and you can get a great deal out of the others in the group – but you have to work quite hard to do it.

Coping with small groups

It's funny but small groups have problems too. In each session there can be a tension as you get to know each other very well and you may not like what you see. You can't hide. There may be the Bertie character who knows it all and answers all the questions. There may be a keen and dedicated student who shows everyone up. The disorganised student causes frustration because you never know what time she might turn up, and she can be quite unreliable. You are sometimes very glad for the Charlies of this world because they can smooth over difficult situations and help everything along for the group. It's too bad if someone's off sick. The group shrinks and the discussions can go very flat.

You are likely to get a lot of tutorial support with such a group size, but you may have to work hard and be very committed. Your opinions will be sought more often and you will all be expected to contribute. Use the support you are given and try to be tolerant of your colleagues.

What is the ideal size for a group?

This tends to be a personal thing but the text books would argue that 30 is an ideal sized group for teaching. For discussion, smaller groups of six to eight are ideal.

Coping on your course

With all of these pitfalls to consider and contend with you may be forgiven for thinking that your course is going to be nothing but a nightmare. This is just not true. There are many people who are working for you and want you to succeed. So who is on your side?

Help on your side

The teaching staff, librarians, support workers in IT and resources rooms, those members of staff in examination departments and everyone else who deals with you on campus are on your side. That's without your family, friends and partners (plus cat, dog or budgerigar – delete as appropriate). It is assumed that you are on your own side, but the experience of students over many years leads us to believe that often the only one who isn't on your side is **you**. Intrinsic motivation, that which motivates you, gets better results. So work for yourself, but also see who else can help you and let them.

Let's look at the personnel listed and how you can organise your studying campaign.

Teaching staff

This may surprise you but they have your best interests at heart. There may be some who are better than others and some you prefer for a variety of reasons, but do use them **within the limits they set**.

The following are some examples of limits set and what to do and not to do with them:

* If your tutor states that you are welcome to ask questions in a time slot in the lecture, don't nobble them after the lecture when they are rushing for coffee/the loo/the next lecture as they may give you short shrift. Philomena often does this as she is often late and consequently misses crucial aspects of a lecture.

* Ask questions in the lecture – don't feel your question is unimportant or obvious; ask and clarify there and then. (You'd be surprised at how many other grateful students there will be if you ask the question. Don't overdo it though, and make yourself look silly by asking the question that has just been answered, or be like Bertie who asks questions off topic to try and show off.)

* If you want a tutorial and you are advised to book an appointment first, don't just turn up at the tutor's door and expect a rapturous welcome. Tutors, like students, have restricted time. All booked tutorials must be attended or cancelled in good time.

* Come to the tutorial with a written list of questions. This saves your memory and ensures that you cover each point you want.

Remember that a tutorial is dictated by you: you can request the help you want.

* When you have booked an appointment for a tutorial, you will get the best from the teacher as the time has been set aside and his/her mind will be on the subject being discussed. Prunella obediently signs up for tutorials and comes with questions to discuss, but very often she already knows the answers to the questions and just needs her confidence to be boosted.

* If you are given a choice of tutorial sessions which have specific dates and time slots, all technically appropriate for you but personally inconvenient for your social/sleep/moonlighting diary, do try to rearrange within the dates and times slots allocated. Don't expect another to be arranged just for you – this, of course, is Charlie's style, with a smile! In an emergency or sickness situation contact the tutor as soon as you can and discuss the options available.

* Many academic institutions now have e-mail coverage for all staff. You can pose your questions electronically or via the phone. These are good ways of contacting staff from a distance.

There are many ways you can seriously upset your tutors and I'm sure that with a bit of effort and ingenuity you could manage a few, but why waste energy on bucking the system when you can easily make it work for you. Do listen to the advice given to you; it's also a good idea to write down any suggestions offered in case you forget.

Once you have understood the limits, get organised (Philomena please note).

Use a diary to note the following:

* when assessment(s) are due
* all important items on your personal calendar, eg. parties/ children's school and social activities/a family get-together/ job etc
* when you are going to fit in study time
* any instructions from tutorial staff, eg. staff absence at a conference/dates of tutorials.

Then work out your schedule. This will allow you to book tutorials accordingly and, if used, arrange the dates/times of your study syndicate (see *Figures 3.1* and *3.2*).

Monday 9–4 lectures syndicate meets 4.30 prep for tomorrow (phone Mum)	Thursday 9–4 lectures tutorial 1.30–2 (Grandad's birthday)
Tuesday Library am CD ROM booked for 9am 2pm lead seminar — arrgh	Friday Phone re: placement details type up assignment (out with Sam 8pm)
Wednesday 9–1 lectures pm free (Tescos)	Saturday/Sunday 11am–3 (restaurant cover) mustn't be late this week 5 pm–12 (bar)

Figure 3.1: Diary example (a)

Week 1 (uni)	Week 2 (placement)	Week 3 (placement)	Week 4 (placement)	Week 5 (placement)
M Syndicate T Tutorial @ 2 W T F Assignment S Agency 7–3 S Agency 1–9	M Start @ 7!! T W T F S Agency (N) S	M T W Tutor visit T F S Crowd to S Kim's party	M T W Tutor visit T F S Agency (N) S	M T W T F Home w/e S Cousin's S Wedding

Week 6 (uni)	Week 7 (uni)	Week 8 (uni)	Week 9 reading wk	Week 10 (exams)
M T W T Assignment F in today S My birthday S	M T W T Tutorial @ 4 F S Home for w/e S	M T W T F S Agency 7–3 S Agency 1–9	M Syndicate T W T Agency 7–3 F Agency 1–9 S S	M T Exam 1 W Exam 2 T F Party!! S Go to Turkey S Monday!!!

Figure 3.2: Diary example (b)

Other areas to organise:

- gather all relevant handouts together in specific folders relating to subject/module
- note which author(s) your tutor refers to
- make sure you and your syndicate (see later in this chapter and *Chapters 4, 7*) get hold of these authors' books/articles
- tap your tutor's brains. If they say something in a lecture you don't understand, be brave, ask them to explain. If the answer given directs you to another source, don't castigate the tutor for ducking the question. Look it up and learn for yourself.

- Compile a filing system/computerised or on cards/in note-book or wherever most helpful. Include in it useful references/quotes/questions to be asked/bright ideas for assignments etc.
- always write your references in full so you don't have to repeat the search
- follow all the tips listed later in this book (see *Chapter 7*).

Deadlines: You will be putting so much work into university led assessment that it would be silly to miss deadlines for handing the work in and suffering the consequences. Make sure that you know how and where to submit your work. Also make sure you read (and question if you don't understand) the rules relating to extensions of time for work, or presenting extenuating circumstances. The information might be found in a student handbook or similar booklet.

Librarians

First find your library. We're surprised at how many students share our allergy of going into a library. We expect the reasons why are very different. Part of our problem is that we are likely to be approached by students asking, 'Can I just...'. By far the greatest problem is getting out again. First you see a book that you must look at (not remotely linked with the assignment in hand, but infinitely more interesting), then you want to look at a whole shelf of books, or else the one you want is missing and you have to order it.

How to use your librarians

1. Be nice to them, smile, say please/thank you – it works wonders for all staff everywhere.
2. Try to be specific in your request, 'The pink and grey book with some black writing on the front' is not very helpful.
3. Try to be intent on a purpose when you go to the library: I am looking at journal articles for my next assignment. The journal must be less than a year old.
4. Take your reading list with you to the library so that you can select from several books the one which suits you. Don't give yourself mental indigestion by taking too many books. Also, be fair to others needing the same books.

5. When requesting advice write down the answers, you may forget. Take note of the full reference/classification numbers, so that you can trace what you want later if necessary.
6. Read any instructions listed around the library before queuing to ask the question already answered for you, eg. this photocopier does not accept cash – use a card that can be purchased from...
7. Tell of your successes so that those who have helped you can be pleased about your results.

    Don't forget that libraries are places for **quiet** study.

IT/practical laboratory/resources support staff

These are very knowledgeable people and are employed to help you.

Why might you need them? They may be able to supply you with the tools for projects, seminars and assignments. They may have examples of previous work available that you may be able to read to help you with your quest.

If you are computer illiterate or phobic, they may be able to help you overcome these problems. Try to arrange a time for personalised help and support. Try to do this early on in your course so that the practicalities of producing your work will not be a greater burden to you than formulating the work itself.

Many campuses have facilities for reduced price disks/paper etc – don't pay over the top unnecessarily. Enquire in the department or campus shop.

The 'Resources Department' in many universities can also include the loan/purchase of equipment for presentations and seminars. A visual aid is so helpful for any presentation and helps focus your mind and that of the audience. Facilities for binding work are usually found in one of these departments. The support personnel of these departments may also be able to assist you with the layout of data in an assignment and help you with binding your work.

Dyslexia

On a different subject, some students have dyslexia. If you suspect that you have dyslexia of words or numbers do seek help or support from the appropriate department in your university. Before any concessions can be made you will have to be 'statemented' by an educational psychologist. This costs money, but universities often have funds to cover this. You will often find that you have to apply to 'student support services' for the advice and support you need in this area. Most tutors are not specifically trained to deal with dyslexia, and associated problems may present themselves in many and varied ways. You need the experts. Once statemented you may be eligible for extra time in exams, enabled to borrow specific equipment and given specialised help.

Friends/family/spouses/partners/pets/others

We are sure all the above are on your side, but this sentiment obviously applies two ways. Many people have stressful lives and it's no good expecting to be centre stage at all times. Give and take on both sides will usually ensure that when you are very stressed prior to an assignment deadline, you will get the support required. Don't forget that good prior planning will help to reduce your stress.This prior planning must also include leisure time.

This support may not always be available when you share accommodation with others who are all handing in work at the same time. Support may then have to come from further afield.

Arrange a syndicate or study group to work with. Use each other. Decide which articles you are going to collect; maybe take it in turns to do a CD ROM search in the library and then share the photocopying costs. Get a selection of recommended texts from the library between you. Arrange meetings to discuss findings. Remember, many assignments ask for analysis and further depth: in a group each of you will view things from a slightly different angle – discuss these differences and you will then get a better analytical picture. Discuss your solutions to the problem and you then find you have begun to synthesise the information. (A high level of cognitive skill can be developed over a cup of coffee.)

Working in a self-formed group/syndicate

Gibbs (1994) wrote a manual containing the following ten pieces of advice to help students work in teams effectively:

1. Be clear what the project is all about – check components, deadlines, assessment.
2. Be selective about who you work with – size, relationships, strengths/weaknesses.
3. Take the trouble to build a real team.
4. Decide how you'd like the team to be, ie. the ground rules.
5. Make sure that someone is doing it, ie. jobs in team – leader, secretary, progress-chaser.
6. Divide the project up and share it out: what? time needed? who?
7. Have proper meetings, not disorganised chats – have a checklist of goals.
8. Discuss how it's going – what, if anything, is going wrong with the team?
9. Give each other feedback, gently (see section on peer assessment, *Chapter 5, pp.64–65).*
10. Plan your team presentation or other activity carefully.

Some people reading this may be mature students who feel torn both ways in that their children are taking exams at the same time. This is obviously a very difficult and trying time for all concerned. There is no comfort in being told that you will all laugh about it later. These crisis times have to be planned for. Household tasks may not get done or , if they are, to a lesser standard than usual. The family may either grow a junior cook or subsist on takeaways for a couple of weeks – but **you will survive**. Try to minimise outside events which are stressful and plan for a treat for everyone at the end.

Examinations department/registrar's office/ faculty office

These all have different areas of responsibility depending on your university. Yours may have additional or combined departments. Key points to remember:

* They normally keep to office hours (9.00am–5.00pm or thereabouts) and could possibly close for lunch. If, for whatever reason, you need to visit outside those hours – ring (or possibly e-mail) first and ask what arrangements can be made; this does save time. Don't just turn up and have a tantrum if they can't deal with your problem right away.

* To get the best out of any department make sure that you have selected the correct one for your enquiry, for example, transcript/ repeat letter of results/new card with university number (you lost the old one).You should always have your university details to hand, such as your student number and any other pertinent data.You will get less overall help if you are vague and disorganised than if you ask your questions clearly and concisely.

Who's on you side if you fail

We like to emphasise success at your studies but we do realise that we fail at times. Failure does not necessarily mean the end of the course.

Failure is often covered by a variety of euphemisms – referred/ deferred, unsuccessful on this occasion. However the word is dressed up, it doesn't help much what it's called, but what the consequences are. So if it happens to you, scream and shout, cry and curse, blame and bemoan but then calm down and face the facts:

1. It's happened.

2. It's not the end of the world (even if it feels like it is).

3. In most cases you can re-do the work – now or at a later date.

Take action. Find out:

1. Why you have failed. If written down read the feedback. If verbal, write down what is said to you, so that you can absorb it later after the shock has subsided.

2. What you need to do to put things right (write it down).

3. What future help is available to you, tutorial times etc.

4. When can you re-submit/re-sit? (note this in your diary).

Now work out a plan of action to achieve second time round (see *page 37*).

However painful, failure is a very valuable learning experience, so don't be too disheartened. After the event many people have told us that they have learned more through the failure than previous successes.

New message to:

Bertie.Brilliance@cerebral.ac.uk

Thanks for the tip about this book. I think it might be very useful. I have just arrived at Medulla Mansions and have had loads of info. Got to get myself around the campus and get organised. They say that everyone wants to help you on the course but will try them out to see if it's true. We'll hear all about different types of theoretical assessment next – not too much I hope. I'm joining lots of societies to try and avoid too much work. Let me know how you're getting on. Charlie

4
Practical/practice-led assessment — who's on your side?

Help with study and assessment related to practice

Your practical assessment may involve being watched directly (observed assessment) or it may mean being questioned or asked to produce written evidence such as a care plan/care study reflection about an incident or a referenced supportive account of an action you have taken (non-observed assessment). The style of your observed assessment may also vary:

- a one-off assessment of a facet of your practice
- a more advanced assessment of a series of skills applied over a period of time, eg. a morning's work
- continuous assessment of your practice, to achieve learning outcomes or competencies.

There are a variety of people on your side, and it is wise to enlist their support. They are:

- staff in your clinical area
- tutorial staff
- family and friends
- you.

This section will concentrate on the **observed assessment** and how to get through.

Being watched directly when assessed in practice is often daunting. It can cause more sleepless nights, make you think more about your practice and produce more specific questions about what is required than written assessment ever does. However, the overriding concern of assessment of practice seems to be the fact that someone is going to watch you perform.

Let's think about this a little – what about people watching us? Patients/clients watch us, as do their relatives or friends, but when it comes to a qualified person watching, there seems to be some apprehension built into the situation. Actually being watched by an assessor can vary because the assessor can just stand/sit and watch and listen, or they can work alongside or with you and watch and listen as you go along.

Whatever the assessor does in the context of your practice should be appropriate for the assessment. The assessor will not start out with the view of, 'I want to fail you'. On the contrary, they will be on your side and keen for your success. Therefore they will be watching for all the correct things you will be doing, not to pounce on the mistakes.

It might sound strange to say this but there actually can be disappointment in assessment of practice if someone does not watch you but still completes your assessment form. Non-observation can raise two questions:

1. How does the assessor know how well you did if they did not watch?
2. How do you know how well you did?

We therefore require someone to observe our performance. This can make you feel very nervous. Recognising the areas of insecurity and identifying them and then discussing them, can often lead to a confident observed assessment even though, due to the concentration and heightened tension, your hands shake. It will be Bertie who needs to recognise the importance of being watched.

So, let's prepare for the assessment of practical skills by looking at the process and the assessor's expectations. The process of assessment of practice is referred to here as the mechanics. The following discussion will look at preparation for assessment in any instance and also preparation for the assessment that is arranged.

The mechanics of observed practical assessment

Certain things should occur before, during and after the performance of a practical assessment. Look out for them, expect them or ask for them if they have not occurred. Before the assessment you should have:

Been taught about the areas of assessment

This teaching may occur in the form of principles or procedures that you are advised to apply and practise. You may have been taught in university or clinical practice.

Discussed the areas of assessment

Lack of information about the assessment is like playing a game without the rules. Imagine playing a card game without any instructions. You are likely to lose and also most probably upset your fellow players. So, in assessment you need to find out the rules so that you do not upset the patient/client, yourself or your assessor.

Had the chance to be involved in the activities that you are going to be assessed on

Being involved in the activities of assessment can mean various stages:

- watching and observing others first, just to see how it is done
- performing part of the activity but having the opportunity to ask for guidance on some or all of the actions
- performing the actions without guidance (see *Chapter 2*).

Had the chance to practise

The amount of practice you require may vary from another student but it is up to you to request the practice that you need. Remember that this practice may involve the actual skill or it may involve the learning of the theory related to the practice. Charlie doesn't often ask to practise something, he feels he can just give 'something a go'. This does not mean that he is always successful – far from it.

Always ask for some guidance on the amount of knowledge that you require. There is no point in learning all the 12 facts related to your practice if only four of them are considered appropriate for the particular assessment you are undertaking. Always be guided by your assessment tool, this may be found in an assessment pro forma, a book of skills, continuous practical assessment documents or the practical assessment criteria given to you for assessment purposes.

Had a chance to ask questions

Many students feel that they need to speak directly to the person assessing them to find out exactly the 'what and how' of their practical assessment. However, this information should be available from any of the tutorial staff/qualified staff in your area of practice. If you find that you have areas of particular concern write your question down in order to remember to ask the assessor. Don't forget to write the answer down as well. Sometimes it is confusing because not everyone does a skill in the same manner. There is not always a 'right' answer but there is usually a principle that you need to know and to apply.

One question you should make sure of asking your assessor is 'Are they willing to participate in the assessment'? That is, will they help you if you need specific assistance.

So, ask and prepare. Like others you will suffer some degree of tension and anxiety due to the pending assessment, but this apprehension is natural. All of us are anxious if we are going to be watched — even famous actors can be anxious before going on stage — but this anxiety can be turned to our benefit. Anxiety to a certain degree can make us sharper, more aware of our surroundings and importantly, more aware of our actions. Think of the increase in blood flow to those vital organs, especially the brain. Surely that is all set to improve your performance.

In the assessment of practice you have to prove that you are **safe**, which means you have to be able to justify your actions. You may be questioned by the assessor about the particular way that you went about an action in the assessment. If you can justify that action in a rational way then it can be accepted.

How to help yourself

Our best advice to you is to find out about the assessment, observe others, practise and ask others to watch and comment on your action. Don't be like Bertie who professes to know it all so does not practise, but likes to challenge the 'whys' and 'wherefores' of other's actions. Philomena is too disorganised to manage any initiative and has to be constantly guided. Charlie, on the other hand, has a go at practice then laughs and jokes about any of his mistakes, taking little heed of the feedback given to him. Not surprisingly, Prunella conscientiously tries to apply any advice she is given and to apply theory to practice.

Another important fact with assessment is that if someone has taken the time to watch and comment on your actions, positively or negatively, then they are showing you respect and importance. You are worth the time and the information. Let them know that you do appreciate the comments, the time and the knowledge that they have tried to impart. You then need to respond to both the positive and the negative elements of their information.

Knowing the time of the assessment means that you can prepare in other ways as well.

Preparing for pre-arranged practical assessment

Finding out about the assessment and practising have been covered, but physically preparing yourself is important. The following may seem like an excerpt from your parents' repertoire but it does help.

Physical preparation

Sacrificing your social activities for the night before an assessment can seem hard but if the assessment only has to be done once there is a benefit to it. Also there are 364 other nights in the year for social activities, give or take a few for assessment purposes. An early night or a restful evening can give you good preparation for your assessment. This preparation should not just include the resting of the body but also the brain. If you do not know it the night before the assessment, be it theory or practice, you won't know it on the day. In fact, last minute 'panic' revision can confuse knowledge on the day. You might remember the book in which you read something but not exactly what you read.

Some students do need this last minute reassurance of ploughing through the books on the night before, but it is best avoided where possible. For someone like Philomena, this would make the situation even worse. Avoid it by the planned approach you have taken prior to the date.

Mental preparation

Rest your brain by doing something unrelated to the assessment. Watch a video or read a book and don't feel guilty. However, don't get too engrossed and stay up too late.

Although we suggest rest of body and brain, a walk or a sports game can have the benefit of relieving the tension and relaxing the mind and body. Tension can be released, especially if it can be taken out on the squash ball. But don't overdo it, you do not want your practical assessment to be compromised by aching muscles that do not allow you to bend or move freely.

Nutritional preparation

Eat and drink both the day before and on the day of the assessment.

Often you do not feel like eating due to the knot in your stomach. Nevertheless, it is important to sustain yourself. Maslow (1971), in his theory of hierarchy of needs, states that physical needs require fulfilment before you can progress to self-actualisation, in other words, successful achievement of the assessment. But do eat with caution – not heavy, stodgy meals that are going to make you feel lethargic.

If you find that eating is beyond you as your stomach seems to be too close to your vocal chords then we advise a drink. This might seem an invitation to visit your local bar but we mean a drink that will be nutritious and which will counteract the acid level in your stomach. Think of milk. We know that you are aware of the fact that although alcohol dilates blood vessels, which might be good to increase the blood supply to the brain, it also has a dulling effect. Any alcohol needs to be taken in moderation, but none before an assessment.

A suggested menu	Rationale
Breakfast Orange juice Cereal One piece of toast	Vitamin C — healthy Lots of goodies A touch of carbohydrate — a treat with marmalade for energy
Coffee One cup with a biscuit	Help with the acidity created by stress
Lunch Cup-a-soup Cheese or egg sandwich Banana and a chocolate bar	To warm the cockles Protein for body building For potassium — it helps nerve conduction and a treat
Evening meal Pasta, a protein based sauce and a salad Apple crumble and custard	Not a heavy meal but a balanced one Would much prefer chocolate cake and cream but the extra carbohydrates tend to have a slight sedentary plus a weighty effect

Think about the things that you are going to need for the assessment

Clean clothes/uniform plus a pen (that works) and the appropriate equipment for the job. Do not wait until the night before, or the morning of the assessment, to discover that you have no suitable clothes. You will have a lot to think about on the actual day so remove some of the anxiety by writing down what you need several days beforehand and collect it together.

So, now it's the day of the assessment. Don't **panic**. Remember you have had the time to panic. Let's look at PANIC in a new light:

You have had time to:

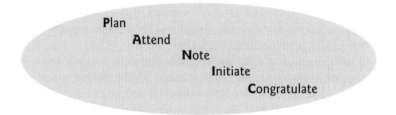

Plan Attend **N**ote Initiate **C**ongratulate

Plan: You have found out when and what your assessment is about.

Attend: You have attended sessions concerning the subject of your assessment or you have requested the help and guidance that you need.

Note: You have had time to note the expected requirements of the assessment.

Initiate: You have had the chance to initiate the help and guidance that you need and to initiate your chance to practice.

Congratulate: This might seem a bit early, as it's prior to the actual assessment, but you can congratulate yourself on your achievements prior to the assessment based on the feedback your mentor/helpers have given you. Take some comfort in the fact that you can do what the assessment requires before you start the actual assessment.

Punctuality

Set the alarm or set several: do not rely on just one source. The assessor has most probably done the same. It is in the assessor's role that they have to see what you are doing so they should be present for the assessment for the required time. An assessment cannot start until he/she is there.

However, do not feel that you have failed the assessment if, after taking all precautions, you are late for no reason of your own — discuss this with your assessor. Each situation will be viewed separately and decided on their unique issues. Be careful if you are late and have rushed that you do not run head first into the assessment situation before you have had time to catch your breath. In the assessment you must think safely, if you are flustered this may not be the case. So take a deep breath, then head for the assessment venue, composed and ready to think logically.

Finally, the day has come when you can demonstrate your skills, your knowledge and your attitude to the situation that will allow you to progress through your chosen course.

It's often not as bad as you have anticipated, but it's a good thing that you have anticipated it and prepared for it.

During the assessment

This advice can be followed in any situation when you are aware that you are being assessed.

Plan out what you are going to do and give yourself time to be prepared

You can always make a brief note of the order of occurrences, but you do not have to stick rigidly to this order. However, do not change it, unless in an emergency, without notifying the assessor. Otherwise the assessor may become confused and a confused assessor is not necessarily a 'happy assessor'. Just think of the information, knowledge and expertise that you can communicate to the assessor if you can justify the reason for your change.

Give yourself time to prepare equipment that is needed. The assessor may not always watch you doing this as they can assess whether you have prepared properly during the procedure.

Most of us have been told, 'If only you would stop and think things through it would save you rushing backwards and forwards for things that you have suddenly remembered or things you have suddenly realised you have forgotten'. As you can imagine, Philomena is told this constantly.

Be prepared to adapt to situations

When being assessed you may think that you need the answers to all situations and that you need to respond to each situation in a knowledgeable manner.

Assessment in a practical clinical situation can encounter a variety of issues. You may be able to deal with some issues but there may be a time when a change results in a totally new situation that you have not experienced before. This leads to a position where you need to demonstrate that you can manage the situation but you may not know what to do. You must make an assessment of your capabilities and if you feel that you need to ask for advice in order to be safe, do so. In some assessment situations, if the assessor has to take action in any way in order to make the situation safe then they are obliged to fail you. (Check what constraints you may need to consider.)

However, do not ask endless questions. Question time should have occurred prior to the assessment. You should have already found out the 'ins and outs' of the type of assessment you are undertaking.

If you ask your assessor to help you, if they have agreed to do so before the assessment, then you must give them precise instructions as to how they should participate.

You do not need to look after your assessor during the assessment. Try to forget that they are there watching and get on with the job in hand. The assessor is responsible for making sure that they see what you do or don't do. So, do not feel that you have to open doors for them or provide them with an easy view or a seat. The assessor should observe you 'as a fly on the wall' except when asked to participate by you. Another point to consider is that you do not have to ask the assessor to help, you can ask another member of staff. Do not make yourself uncomfortable if you feel awkward about asking the assessor.

Look after yourself

Some assessments can be long and tiring especially if you did not sleep well the night before and you could not face breakfast because of your anxiety. Think of your breaks and ensure that you sit down for a period and that you eat at suitable intervals. The assessor may be glad to have a break too.

After the assessment

The assessor is required at the end of an assessment to give you some feedback. Often this feedback starts with being asked, 'How do you think you did?' Be prepared for this. You should be in a quiet room, undisturbed and sitting down. Be ready to make a self-assessment. You might think that this self-assessment is the assessor making you do their work but, in fact, it is a very important aspect of assessment (see *Chapter 5*). Self-assessment demonstrates your awareness of how you have performed. It demonstrates your knowledge of the procedures and practices that you have carried out. It allows you to raise your concerns about possible occurrences during the assessment. Discussing these with your assessor demonstrates your concern but it also allows for an important aspect of assessment: the help and guidance towards future practice. Assessment should help to develop you as a practitioner and as a person. There is always something else to be learnt or even remembered from previous knowledge. It seems a pity that we cannot remember everything that we have learnt all of the time. But, like a computer there can be 'insufficient memory' and as we get older this seems to get worse – now, where was I?

Yes, I remember. Listen to your assessor, welcome their advice, their comments. Don't look on the discussion points as criticism in a negative manner but look on them as a 'thank you for spending the time to tell me, and yes, I will learn. I know I have to gain knowledge and experience from all sorts of sources and this feedback is one source'.

How to make your assessor's day

This is not done by chocolate and/or flowers but by enabling them to say 'well done' at the end of your assessment because you have put everything into the assessment and really demonstrated your best knowledge, skills and attitudes. You have been a credit to yourself.

Have you ever had to or stopped to think what it is like to say to someone, 'I am sorry but...'. In healthcare there are many instances when a sentence may start with those words. The various situations are a difficult time for the speaker and the listener as those words are often a prelude to a sad situation.

Assessors find that having to fail students is a hard decision, a decision that is not taken lightly. It may also be a decision that is reflected on for several days after giving the result. It is much better for the assessor if they can say 'well done, although there might be one or two points that need discussion/attention'.

This discussion should be taken in the context it is given. The assessor is giving you his/her evidence of observation from the assessed situation as well as expert opinion/advice. What the assessor is saying is not there to be disputed. If you are going to deny or object to some of the comments then you are going to miss the points being made (Bertie is guilty of this). In fact, you cannot dispute what the assessor said did or did not happen, you can only object if the assessor's conduct during the assessment was a problem to you.

Listen to the assessor and take on board their comments (a word in Charlie's ear). The comments will in part be congratulatory if you have passed, but they will also include points to be considered for future use. We all need to continually grow and develop; the assessor in his/her feedback is giving you some pointers. Philomena should benefit from points about her organisation and should not be pre-occupied with the next thing she hasn't yet prepared for.

So prepare well, perform well and acknowledge guidance well – the assessor will appreciate that. Equally, you will appreciate the step forward you make in your progress; it works both ways.

Preparing for the non-arranged continuous assessment

This can involve most of the advice given for the arranged assessment except for the important difference that you do not know when. So:

- be prepared
- be aware of what you might be assessed on
- perform as you should do each day
- be safe.

Be prepared

Preparation for non-arranged assessment starts at the initial interview on commencement of a placement experience.

During the initial interview with your mentor/assessor you should:

1. Find out the opportunities that are available to you while on the experience.

2. Be able to discuss your unique requirements.

3. Work out your intended outcomes/objectives.

4. Draw up a programme for achievement.

Be aware of what you might be assessed on

What you are going to be assessed on should be identified in your programme for achievement. Be prepared to be assessed on the practical aspects linked to your course programme for achievement.

Make sure that this links with any practical assessment documentation you are provided with.

Perform as you should do each day

This is good practice for being assessed at any time. However, first find out what you should do.

Ask someone, watch someone, and then ask to perform with someone watching you and commenting on how you are performing. Be sure you are doing things right. All of these activities need to occur during the first half of your time in an area of practice. The reason for this is that at the half-way stage you will be given assessment feedback, formative assessment, that will let you know how you are progressing and the improvements you might need to make. During the second half of your placement you will be expected to continue with good practice that may be assessed at any time. So keep practising, ask to do things, get yourself involved. The more you practise, the more you learn. Bertie, take note, you may know the theory but application in practice is a different matter. Do not just do something once, try at least four to five times as the opportunity arises.

Be safe

This is an important aspect to consider. We can often try and do something by trial and error and end up with the correct result (a survival tactic of Charlie's). However, in the trial and error experience we may have done something unsafe. Consider trying to drive without instruction; some people can manage the car but are unsafe on the road with other traffic or suddenly realise that they cannot handle the situation when the traffic lights are changing to red just as they are approaching at speed. Alternatively, you may not be able to achieve the outcome. 'Fudging an issue' is not an acceptable course of action.

However, with patient/client care we need to be more careful. It's not a case of experimentation to see if you can manage the care that is required. Imagine a doctor having to remove a cyst or even perform any other surgical procedure on you who starts with the comment, 'Well I am not sure how its done, or I have only seen it done once, but here goes'. Worse still, if the doctor refers to a book for guidance.

Remember in the non-arranged assessment that you need to show that you are safe at all times. It is important that you recognise what you know you can do accurately and what you are not sure of. Anything you do not know, you must ask. This does not go against you in your assessment. In fact it can work the opposite for you as it could demonstrate that you are a keen and safe student.

The student who asks, wants to learn

This student will come across as interested, motivated and worthy of help. Prunella is always asking relevant questions and finds she gets a lot of support. Bear in mind though that asking for help may mean that you are advised to do some work on your own. If you want to find out about something in particular, you might be advised about it and where to get supplementary information. Doing this work on your own is not a 'cop out' for the person you have asked as they should discuss your findings with you after you have had time to gain the information. Make sure that you arrange a follow-up time to discuss your findings; be there and be ready, Charlie and Philomena.

Non-arranged/continuous assessment means that for a longer period of time you are not only being assessed but you are having more contact with your assessor. We have to add the word hopefully as a rider, because we recognise the problems of busy clinical areas, shortages of staff and different shift patterns. Often a criticism of non-arranged/continuous assessment from the student's perspective is that there is little opportunity to work with the assessor. Contact with your assessor should work to your benefit, particularly if you have confidence and respect for your assessor and they are what you would refer to as a 'good role model'. If you want to emulate your assessor then the relationship can be helpful. However, if your assessor does not possess every quality that you would like them to have, then the whole process can create problems.

Dealing with the problem of dissatisfaction with your mentor/assessor can be stressful in itself. Determine if you are the problem.

Suggested coping mechanisms are:

Identify the problem in concrete terms

For example, you may not feel happy with the manual handling procedure that the assessor uses and find that you certainly will not follow their lead or you are not keen on the attitude conveyed when elderly patients/clients are being treated.

'Concrete terms' means that you must then state exactly what was done or said, the actual fact. You might not like the way that the assessor talks to you but you need to state the exact conversation. Having identified the problem/s then you need to take some action while you are in the situation. Do not leave it until you have left the area as the next student will most probably have the same stressful experience that you have had. Remember that learning and assessment are ongoing life-long developments. This involves not just you but your mentor/assessor as well so make sure that the situation is dealt with to help all the parties involved.

Raise the problem

1. If you feel that you can talk to your mentor/assessor then do so at a convenient time. Not when the area is busy and they are just going to do something important.
2. If you feel uncomfortable talking to your mentor/assessor then talk to someone else you do feel comfortable with. This could include the clinical area's manager, a colleague or a member of the tutorial staff.

Do not let the problem/s go on

This does not give you an open invitation to go around reporting those people who you feel are poor mentors/assessors. There must be some self-assessment on your part to see if some of the problem is originating from yourself. For example, if you are not showing any interest in the work in the clinical area, trying to avoid every practical procedure offered then the mentor/assessor may have some problems with you. Also, if they try to give advice/correction and you are not too keen on taking it, then they can feel thwarted in their attempt to help you.

The best advice would be to try and get along with your mentor/assessor. It is a valuable experience to prepare and enable you to manage the people/staff/patients/clients that you will encounter in your working career and, of course, in your personal life. Use the mentor/assessor relationship to find out more about yourself as a person and how you come across to others; and how to manage and work and live with others. Not always an easy task, but learn from it. However, as mentioned above, do use help if needed. Sometimes your colleagues/peers may help you too.

New message to Bertie:

Bertie.Brilliance@cerebral.ac.uk

I can see there are several lessons I should learn from this chapter. The one that especially comes to mind is not to PANIC. I am going to work on that. I will do a plan in my diary — that is when I find it! Also, it does emphasise that we all should make good use of practical experience — I must get organised and not be late.

Philomena

5
Peer and self-assessment

This chapter will look at two forms of assessment which although 'formative' can help you to succeed at summative assessment.

Peer assessment

Peer assessment can raise many questions:

- what is meant by 'peers'?
- what right do they have to assess me?
- are they going to give an accurate or biased assessment?
- am I going to feel comfortable with them giving me assessment feedback?
- isn't it bad enough that I have to be assessed by qualified staff without my peers being able to comment as well?

None of these questions seem to put a positive light on the fact that peers may assess you. So, let's look at these questions more closely.

Defining the term 'peer' does not entirely give us a clear answer. The *Oxford English Reference Dictionary* (1995) says that a peer is, 'a person who is equal in ability, standing, age, rank or value'. Let's consider the words in this definition.

Equal in ability

Although general guidelines of academic ability are stipulated for your course not every one will have an identical range. Also, the practical or life experiences of your peers may vary tremendously. No two people are exactly the same. We all have our own qualities, good and bad. Peer assessment should use the good qualities of one to aid the poor or developing qualities of another, for example, Bertie's knowledge and Prunella's practical skills could both complement their course colleagues.

Standing

What about standing? Yes, all peers should be equal in standing. However, how often do you put yourself down as not being as good as another, or consider yourself to be better than others? Standing is often self-inflicted by your own interpretation of your value or worth to the group. For example, Bertie's air of self-importance and Philomena's awareness of her chaotic lifestyle.

Age

Let's hope that whatever the age of your peers they can contribute something, ie. a fresh perspective, vitality, experience or a critical eye — meant in the most helpful of terms. A person with a critical eye can often recognise potential problems because of his/her previous life experience.

Rank

Your peers are all recognised to be at the same level or rank, for example, a first year student. However, some do generally appear more confident/responsible than others. You might actually unofficially rank yourself against your peers. Often unjustifiably when you state you are not as good. For example, Prunella with her struggles in theoretical work might compare herself unfavourably against Bertie.

Value

All students are valued whatever you may think. Often in placement settings students might feel that they are only a pair of hands and no one is bothered with them. It's possible that you need to look at your own assessment of the situation and determine whether you value yourself. If you do not value yourself then you are unlikely to feel valued by others: with this viewpoint you can make it difficult for others to convince you that you are valued. Taking constructive criticism in a negative way can often make you feel devalued.

Hopefully from these discussions it can be seen that peer assessment is a positive aspect of assessment. It is about you assessing others and others assessing you.

How can peer assessment help you?

Assessment is about finding out from a multitude of sources how you are progressing in your course.

Peers can be said to be more:

- lenient in their assessment
- realistic
- in-depth, as they know you better or there has been more contact over a longer period of time
- on your side because it is their side as well.

What right do peers have to assess you?

Actually the answer to this could be none. What gives one person the right to comment on another? Why should peers assess you? But, from a positive angle there are many advantages to peer assessment, for example:

- it can be given informally in a variety of situations
- it makes assessment more informal and therefore more acceptable and understandable to help you recognise your potential
- it helps you and your peers recognise your learning needs
- it is more accessible, more frequent than clinical/tutorial assessment
- it develops your confidence in your skills, knowledge and attitudes
- it allows you to help others
- it encourages you to be more objective about situations in practice.

Is peer assessment going to give an accurate or biased assessment?

This question is relevant to any form of assessment by anyone. So many factors can influence others' judgement of our performance. Peer assessment may give very accurate assessment because your peers may know you quite well. They may be able to recognise factors such as your anxiety, for example, the change in your voice or the expression on your face, which would not necessarily be obvious to someone who does not know you. The accuracy of this assessment can at times be difficult to deal with especially if the person is a close friend. It is worth dealing with this assessment as a guide to changes/ adaptations you may need to make but allow it to let you become more aware of yourself. Remember we all have various idiosyncrasies. These idiosyncrasies may be the factors that our peers like and feel they can point out. So do not take offence at them, but use the pointers as helpers. Being told that you are pedantic may not be a criticism it may be a quality your peers admire in you and rely on.

However, be aware of the instances when the assessment can be of a destructive nature. This can be seen in the verbal bullying that goes on. Assessment from peers that hurts, that seems unkind, should be treated in the same light as the poor results of assessment from assessors. You should query it with the person or ask for other advice. You do not just have one peer so ask other peers to help in giving you a more balanced view of the assessment of your performance.

Beware that your peers can be too kind, they can be biased. Your friend may only be giving you the advice/feedback they know you want to hear or that they think you need to be able to perform the assessment. This kindness and support can help you with your confidence so take some of this possibly biased assessment and use it to give you confidence.

Beware of always disagreeing with any form of peer assessment. What is the purpose of asking if you do not listen and take some heed of the comments made? Peer assessment should not provoke an argument.

Are you going to feel comfortable with giving/receiving assessment feedback?

This is most probably the hardest part of peer assessment, as peer assessment does not necessarily mean you are always receiving comment but you are giving comment too. How do you tackle the problem of telling a friend that her assignment or an area of her practice is no good? This is even more complicated when you know she is extremely anxious and her relationship with her boyfriend has just ended and she is very close to tears. Do you tell her the work is 'alright' or how do you constructively tell her the changes that she needs to make? You will obviously bear in mind that you cannot actually do the work for her, which is often a temptation when you see a friend struggling.

Often the answer is to give only the positive points – but do learn how to convey the points that require improvement. Pointing out areas for improvement can help you develop; in giving these comments you have to clarify your knowledge and ensure that, as far as you know, you are giving the correct advice. Teaching or helping someone helps you to learn but it also can indicate the areas of help you need. So use it jointly.

Balancing feedback from your peers and mentors/assessors

Sometimes you might feel more comfortable with some of your peers and their comments. You might find that you understand their comments better than the qualified assessor. It is worth remembering that their comments are adding to the picture that you are getting of yourself. Sometimes their comments will be given on an individual basis and in private where you can digest them more easily.

Ground rules of peer assessment

You must be fair with each other and agree what you are commenting on and how.

In a formal setting this will be determined by the tutor organising the event, such as a seminar. The more informal assessment just discussed highlights the need for:

- co-operation
- being comfortable with each other
- constructive criticism – given and taken
- comments that are kind but which also point out the weak areas
- commitment to help and support.

New message to:

CharlieAvLazy@medullamansions.net
Frantic.Philomena@internetrush.UK
BertieBrilliance@cerebral.ac.uk

I hope you are all reading and taking notice of what this book is saying. I can see why all the effort put into to our courses will not be wasted. We need to pull together and help each other a bit more. Sorry I've been concentrating on my own work so much.
Your 'peer'
Philomena

Self-assessment

Self-assessment should eliminate the problem of unreliability in assessment as it is you and you alone assessing yourself. In other words you state what you have learnt, how you have learnt it and what else you need to learn. You also need to consider how you will make up your deficits and what will demonstrate your learning achievement.

A lot of decisions, but these will put you firmly in the driving seat of your learning. However, you will only become the reliable driver/critic of your learning if you find out the rules.

Rules of learning: the what and how

What: has to be learnt?
        are the resources?
        are the time limits?

How: do you best learn?
        can you demonstrate your learning?

It means you have to find out what you need to learn and also discuss whether the proof/evidence is going to be sufficient to meet the requirements. In other words, you need some guidance so search out your guide, ie. a tutor, a qualified practitioner or appropriate friend, and discuss your strategy.

Your learning strategy should give you the 'what' and 'how' of learning listed above, preparing a timetable to work to and identifying the resources you need to use. (This is sometimes called a 'learning contract'.)

Remember, your timetable must suit you. If you are not good at achieving deadlines, then set them earlier than required. Alternatively, if you realise that you are too intense in your work and that you spend all hours looking up all sorts of information, much of which is irrelevant, get advice from someone who is good at summarising your thoughts.

One of the important aspects of self-assessment is the admission of 'I don't know'. Then, seek out the answers. As a qualified practitioner in the future you are going to be responsible for your work, so you must learn to identify where you have knowledge and skills and can perform safely and where you must seek help and guidance.

You will constantly be assessing your own work as a practitioner so make it part of your learning as a student. You need to develop self-awareness that you feel comfortable with, in which you know you perform safely and where you recognise your limitations. In future not only will you assess your own work but that of students and/or other staff.

Setting about self-assessment

What has to be learnt?

This can be determined from the aims and objectives of your course or sections of the course. This is often the literature that you are given on the first day, the material that is sometimes filed but not necessarily read. Another source for what has to be learnt is the briefing guidelines of theoretical work and the practical assessment documentation. Determining what is to be learnt can be problematic. You need to clarify the learning required. Write down the requirements in your own words and ensure with your assessor that you have a correct understanding right from the start. If you do not have a clear idea of the expectation you will be working in the dark and possibly come out with the wrong result.

What are the resources?

In other words, what are you going to need and what is going to help you. Each student is an individual and will require different assistance: so, assess your own personal requirements.

Look at the environment you are in and what is available. Practical areas have the equipment and realistic situations for you to develop some skills. Remember practice makes perfect so use this resource. Ask to see, ask to do with supervision, ask to be assessed – these should be familiar words by now.

Develop the use of a computer if you are a novice. Do not necessarily shy away from it but ask to be taught to use the word processing side first. It may save you a lot of time and if you are poor at spelling and grammar the computer may be your saving grace as it can do a spell and grammar check for you. Be brave, plunge in and use the resources. If you are an expert, do your assignment work first and then surf away.

What are the time limits?

It is very important that your study and assessment fits in with your personal life, so check the time limits and make a plan that includes your social life and work to it. This can relieve the panic of assessment (see *Chapter 3*).

How do you best learn?

You need to take a look at yourself and decide how you best learn. There have been several opportunities to do this throughout the book. It may be helpful at this point to visit literature on learning styles and time management (see *Chapter 6*) as the latter could be harder to control when working on your own.

Knowing your strengths and weaknesses in this area will help you use the resources, mentioned above, in a more efficient way.

How can you demonstrate your learning?

The multitude of assessments you could do is discussed in *Chapter 2*. Each type of assessment should demonstrate appropriately the knowledge, skills and attitudes that are needed for a particular purpose. A written account of the operation of a piece of machinery does not necessarily indicate that the person can operate the machine.

With the types of courses Bertie *et al* are studying, there will be a strong link of the theory work with the relevant areas of practice.

Sometimes it would be nice to have a 'wish list' of assignments.

The following set of examples show how our intrepid four have come to terms with some of their strengths and weaknesses and how they plan to overcome some of their weaknesses.

Bertie would like to demonstrate this by working with a group of patients for a day. He will verbally describe the reasons for his care and treatments to the physiotherapist assessor working with him.

Prunella has decided and agreed that she would like to write a case study of a patient using research to demonstrate that her care was evidence-based.

Philomena has decided to challenge herself and has volunteered to organise the students' end of year party. This may not be an actual assignment, but it will demonstrate her commitment to work at something that requires many organisational skills. Recognising that she has not got all the organisational skills necessary, she has enlisted the help of her new boyfriend in this venture.

Charlie has decided to work with several from his group to do a role-play. This will not stretch Charlie too much and in many ways this will be an ideal medium for him. One thing he will have to do is turn up and play his part.

For self-assessment to be effective, the following points need to be remembered. It must be:

- planned
- negotiated between you and your assessor (mentor/tutor)
- appropriate to the intended outcomes
- able to demonstrate the learning at the correct level
- used to develop you.

It must not create a situation where you:

- take the easiest option
- decide at the last minute the approach to take
- complete the university/practice-led assessment without some agreement with the assessor.

In summary to prepare for self-assessment, complete the following steps:

- look at the intended learning outcome(s)
- consider your resources
- assess yourself, areas to be developed
- determine means of assessment
- discuss and agree your approach with your assessor by the date stated in your course (or earlier)
- agree your 'contract'/'action plan'.

Figures 5.1 and 5.2 give an example of how a self-assessment plan could look using an intended learning outcome and an imaginary student.

New message to:

Frantic.Philomena@internetrush.uk
BertieBrilliance@cerebral.ac.uk
Prunella@practicalfreeserve.co.uk

OK guys. It looks like we are all in this together. Let's meet in the holidays and discuss where we are. I know now that I need to take my studies more seriously, the only thing is I am not very good at that as I would rather be out than studying. Can you help me?
Charlie

Reply:

Bertie.Brilliance@cerebral.ac.uk
Frantic.Philomena@internetrush.uk
CharlieAvLazy@medullamansions.net

It's alright for you lot — I don't get long holidays! Prunella

Resources
Clinical/placement area Library for literature on communication Mentor/assessor for advice Colleagues Tutorial staff
Self-assessment
Strengths Outgoing, interested in people, keen to learn practically ***Weaknesses*** Sometimes jump in with both feet Say inappropriate things Try to make a joke of things Lack of knowledge ***Areas to develop*** Listening skills Knowledge about patients'/clients' conditions Consideration before speaking to allow for tactfulness Appropriate responses
Means of assessment Observations of others, introductions, data gathering and discussion of care Reflection on observations with discussion of observation with participant
Write out and agree contract with supervisor/tutor

Figure 5.1: Learning outcome: to communicate effectively with patients/clients

The following contract (*Figure 5.2*) identifies three aspects of communication with patients/clients. These are:

i.   Give advice to patients/clients.

ii. Write an assignment.

iii. Verbally relate information.

Outcome	Resources	Evidence	Date
Communicate effectively with patients/ clients	Tutorial staff	Write contract	1 Feb
	Clinical/place-ment area	Observe four members of staff communicating	8 Feb
	Mentor/assessor	Write up observations and discuss	
		Conduct four con-versations – first a role play	12 Feb 16 Feb– 20 Feb
		i. Give advice to one patient	
		Select patient	18 Feb
		Collect information	22 Feb
	Library/Mentor assessor	Discuss information	26 Feb
		Give advice to patient	1 March
		ii. Write assignment Select topic	4 Feb
	Library CD Rom	Conduct literature search	12 Feb
		Read and make notes	20 Feb
	Tutorial	Write outline	22 Feb
		Write main body	
		1	24 Feb
		2	26 Feb
		3	1 March
		Write conclusion	3 March
	Tutorial staff/IT dept	Prepare seminar	6 March
		Present seminar	10 March
	Clinical/placement area	**iii. Verbally relate information about one patient/client to another member of staff**	
	Mentor/assessor	Select patient	28 Feb
	Colleagues/mentor assessor	Gather information	1 March
		Practice information giving. Give information to another member of staff	8 March

Figure 5.2: A contract related to the outcome in *Figure 5.1*

6

Short cuts to studying, learning and assessment

An overview of available literature – we've read the books for you

There are many books written on the art of assessment from the theoretical perspective. This is a good place from which to start learning how to use the assessment process to the student's advantage. The authors have selected and reviewed a variety of books for you. You can use the review as a short cut to select the book which appeals to you most or get the most out of the sections mentioned. The books selected are mainly divided into sections to facilitate personal study. As can be seen from the reference list, the last ten years have been a time when students have been able to acquire books to help with studying, writing and grammar, examination techniques, learning skills, tips on many subjects and how to survive. Hopefully you will be able to think back to subjects covered in earlier sections of this book

Looking at the theoretical side of the assessment process encompasses a variety of skills. Using the framework of 'assessing, planning, implementing and evaluating', the books on the list will be reviewed. These will naturally follow the pattern of a student considering action before study, during study and after the assessment of study has taken place.

Before study

Assessing

Are you a super student? If the answer is 'yes', then you may be in line for some disillusionment – if the answer is 'no', then you may be realistic but perhaps lacking in confidence. Rowntree (1988) sets the scene by destroying the 'Myth of the Super Student' and sets reasonable guidelines to help the ordinary student cope with study.

The process of theoretical assessment has to start with the individual. Questions such as, 'which learning style do I prefer?' and 'what are my time management skills like?' are important. 'Where do I study, and how can I spread my books conveniently?' are vital questions to prevent domestic disharmony over the studying process.

Using the format devised by Honey and Mumford, learning styles are covered in some detail by Maslin-Prothero (1997), Brown and Hawkesley (1996), Lashley (1995), Gillett (1990) and, to a limited extent, by Murdoch and Davies (1994). It is interesting to note that all but Lashley are writing for nurses and recognise the importance of knowing one's own style as a starting point for studying. Cottrell (1999) emphasises the importance of recognising one's own learning preferences without getting 'stuck into a type', while Race (1992) discusses how students can develop their own methods of determining learning styles.

Time management features in many more books with differing ideas given as to how to manage one's time. The general theme is that it is a skill that needs to be taught and practised. Many people can manage time more than adequately until another problem piles on top. That 'problem' is often the extra work associated with the course work to be completed. The books start by encouraging the student to diagnose the source of the problem and then to sort out what can be done to improve the situation. Maslin-Prothero (1997) suggests that students prepare a list of commitments and other activities, recommending realism and balance to maintain a happy and healthy life (see *page 38* for an example of a student diary). Drew and Bingham (1997) identify very practical ways of dealing with time management problems such as prioritising. Rowntree (1988) focuses on the need to plan in the long term then divide that time up into manageable 'chunks'. Gillett (1990) starts her argument with the need to consider the benefits of delegation and then to look at the time available for the activities that need to be done. Prioritising, again, is a key word here. Lashley (1995) looks at the need for full time students to plan their study time rather than the overall approach to life time management. Goodall (1995) uses a similar approach concentrating on the need to plan for each assignment; doing the background reading, organising tutorial appointments and then word processing the final draft. This format is expanded pictorially in Cottrell's (1999) notes, and she gives a lot of advice about planning specific study assignments.

Cuba and Cocking (1994) refer only briefly to time management while Race (1992) gives ten useful tips stressing that the student is in charge of his/her own time and the possible pitfalls of wasting this time. Northedge (1990) puts time management alongside task management. A useful 'soap opera' style scenario is included which identifies areas in which students can improve their overall study management.

This naturally leads on to the situation of organising the environment in which study should take place. Once again, many of the books look at the physical and emotional environment where study takes place. The essential element is being able to study without interruption, and Taylor (1992) uses cartoons to illustrate this and the need for work to be left undisturbed. This is obviously difficult if the work desk is also the dining room table.

Race (1992) has some marvellous tips for students as to what not to do when approaching study. How to sort out the right task from the procrastinating one and the right environment in which to work. Simple things need to be considered. Maslin-Prothero (1997) lists things like a comfortable chair, room to spread and sufficient light and ventilation as precursors to effective study.

Friendship networks are also advised for the emotional support required to 'keep the student going' while on the course. Lashley (1995) graphically demonstrates the folly of some study positions, bed and armchair lounging being undesirable. On a more serious note, a useful timetable of activities is demonstrated in his and all the other books. A balance of reasonable exercise, diet, sleep and the absence of alcohol during the studying period is recommended by Duncalf (1994).

The student needs to assess how the above suggestions affect his/her studying process and decide which ones to implement. The transition to planning the study should then be made easier.

During study

Planning

Each student needs to refer to the time plan that was produced when looking at the subject of time management. Each module, assignment and relevant commitment needs to be on the plan so that the relevant resources can be organised.

Surprisingly, very few of the books look specifically at the resources students can use to help in the study process. Murdoch and Davies (1994) have a guided study to follow for the specific purpose of literature searching which then goes into some detail as to how to access different aspects of library services. The variety of sources of information in a library is also highlighted. Casey (1993) also looks briefly at the use of libraries.

Lashley (1995) takes a different tack and suggests key questions a student needs to ask relating to the piece of work to be undertaken. Goodall (1995) develops this idea further and stresses the importance of ensuring that the purpose and nature of the assignment is fully understood, which can be added to the list of questions mentioned above. Another key planning consideration is the date by when this piece of work must be completed so that the overall plan can be prepared.

Cuba and Cocking (1994) have a comprehensive section called the management of writing, which includes the use of libraries and relevant tutorial support. They also go into some detail regarding the process of using a library and the literature therein. Gillett (1990) expands on this theme, she lists a variety of other human resources who may be accessed for study. These include the staff on placements, family and peer group support. This book also has a detailed account on how to use sections of a library.

Maslin-Prothero's (1997) book contains three chapters on resources discussing the use of library facilities, information technology, computers in particular, and the staff teaching the course being undertaken. Cottrell (1999) brings the resources issue even more up-to-date when she outlines all the facilities available in a university library. She also highlights the need to check the authority of an internet source. Taylor (1992) looks at some of these subjects in a different way but covers the material just as well.

The student always needs to remember that the teachers encouraging study and requiring assignments do not do this with the aim of causing the student to trip and fall. The purpose is to enable the student to learn and ultimately succeed in the course being undertaken. To that end assignment briefs, reading lists, module learning outcomes and guides, handouts and all the other paraphernalia of teaching, are designed to assist the student. None of these pieces of paper will be of the slightest use if they are just hole-punched and filed. However, Cottrell (1999) advises students where and how to file relevant information when the appropriate time comes.

Once libraries have been accessed and plundered the student needs to get down to some serious reading. This reading needs to encompass course notes from lectures, handouts as well as books and journals on the subject matter.

It is a waste of time for the student to read all this material if the information is not processed correctly in the brain, to enable appropriate writing skills to follow. Many of the books under review itemise ways of effective reading and subsequent note taking. Rowntree (1988) has two excellent chapters on reading alone. In *chapter 5* he outlines the now widely used SQ3R strategy to survey, question, read, recall and review material in a book/journal. Surveying, as well as reading, is a vital skill at the library stage as the reader can select the book(s) which are most likely to suit the needs of the study topic in hand. A brief check of the contents page, and the introduction and conclusion of pertinent sections of the book listed, can determine whether a book is appropriate to be borrowed. Taylor (1992), Lashley (1995), Cottrell (1999) and Gillett (1990) pick up the same theme in their books, each giving some further tips to enable the student to grasp this process. Taylor (1992), for example, has a useful chapter on how to read and critique research. Once again Race (1992) provides some realistic tips that are slightly different from the other texts.

Northedge (1990) takes a more emotional view of reading by looking first at people's feelings towards reading. Several exercises are included in the text to diagnose problems and to help individuals to read more effectively. Casey (1993) shows how to develop existing skills and also encourages leisure reading – a luxury some students may feel too guilty to indulge in. Maslin-Prothero (1997) uses a similar approach but the examples and exercises are very different.

Each book covers the subject of reading adequately in its context but several books (Northedge, 1990; Brown, 1990; Gillett, 1990; Cottrell, 1999; Rowntree, 1988) pick different approaches to this subject which may be considered as a 'natural' exercise.

Not all the books have a section on effective note taking. Several link the process to other activities. Lashley (1995) points out bad practice in lecture note taking while Rowntree (1988) links note taking firmly with the reading process and the 'why, when and ways' of this activity. Northedge's (1990) approach is very thorough and strongly associated with memory.

Drew and Bingham (1997) look at two levels of each subject and here look at where students are starting in the process of note taking and how to develop this skill further. Cottrell (1999) shows some of the many ways and short cuts that can be made through using 'mind maps' or 'pattern notes' when taking and making notes. The remainder (Gillett, 1990; Casey, 1993; Taylor, 1990; Brown, 1990; Goodall, 1995) all include a brief account with similar practical activities to help students with their notes from lectures and written sources. Race (1992) opts for note making versus note taking.

Implementing

For many students the main reason for study is the acquisition of a qualification as a result of successful assignment grades, not necessarily the sheer joy of learning for the sake of it. Assignments, examinations, projects, seminars, reports and critiques are all means by which knowledge can be assessed and graded. These, and having time limits for presentation of this material, also help to concentrate the mind.

This section will be reviewing what the books have to say about the different methods of information presentation. The contents of the books will be reviewed regarding their information about writing assignments, projects, reports, critiques, examination essays and presenting seminars. Few of the books cover every eventuality but a combination of the books will help a student tackle any of these tasks.

The texts written for nurses tend to have the wider range of subjects which are specific for nursing courses. However those more general texts are excellent in their own right in that the principles included can easily be applied to any healthcare university-led study.

Gillett (1990) divides her book into the various assessment sections and advises on specific ways of checking that an assignment has been written correctly. She recommends a check list and specific time management stages. Advice is also given on how to prepare to meet tutorial staff. Seminars are given a similar treatment with additional advice on how to cope with 'nerves' in a presentation. Exam preparation is also included.

The two tier approach of Drew's and Bingham's (1997) book gives a good and complementary series of activities, pointers and direct guidance for the essay writer. They include some good ideas on how to make essays 'flow' and how to develop a logical argument. The additional sections on report writing give insight and examples relating to both research and report writing skills.

The majority of Goodall's (1995) book is taken up with writing skills. There are seven chapters devoted to different types of written assessment and one on oral presentation of a subject. The types of written work range from essay and care study writing to a large-scale project and research critique. There is also a chapter on the unseen examination. His approach is quite simplistic but practical. Useful extras that do not appear in many other texts are items such as how to tackle 'academic' writing skills. Grammar, style and punctuation are also included, and, although not in a vast amount of detail, Goodall discusses the niggling problems many students have.

A book, which looks specifically at grammar, punctuation and spelling, is by Peck and Coyle (1999). It takes the reader through the three stages of writing correctly, writing confidently and then writing with style. It requires a certain amount of discipline to work through this book, but it is written simply and in a non-patronising fashion.

Cocker (1987), Brown (1990) and Duncalf (1994) all write exclusively for successful examination achievement. Cocker and Brown both relate to the school examination process but are adaptable, whereas Duncalf is wide ranging and includes the driving test.

Casey (1993) focuses mainly on essay writing and has a good chapter covering many of the key aspects of essay writing included in the other books. He also includes information on how to put a project together.

The study skills book by Taylor (1992) is similar to, although much briefer than, Gillett's approach. Essay writing is linked closely to referencing with another chapter on projects, seminars and research reports. A third chapter on the subject of written work is on examination techniques.

The nursing text edited by Maslin-Prothero (1997) describes an effective writing style for all types of academic work. A series of principles is given. This particular chapter is enhanced by a later one of using logical argument to develop individual writing skills. A further chapter on advanced writing skills related to portfolio production is also included. For students needing help in writing a logical argument, Cottrell (1999) has a two-page section but the 'using logical argument' theme is also used in Young's (1996) more specialised book on the art and science of writing. She covers all the parts of speech and how to build a sentence. This is usefully developed to discuss the writing of different types of academic work. Definitely a 'how to write book' rather than the more generalised study skills books.

The Good Study Guide (Northedge,1990) has well over 100 pages devoted to different aspects of the various ways of presenting academic writing. Essay writing predominates with a variety of examples for criticism of style and technique. The 'craft' of writing is examined as well as the 'dos and don'ts' of approaching examination answers. 'Making a convincing case' is one of the sections supporting essay writing overall.

Murdoch and Davies (1994) have only a brief section on report writing and how to critically review research reports. Cuba and Cocking (1994) on the other hand have a wide range of entries for differing types of work that need to be produced within the social sciences field. A writing strategy is the first thing recommended, then the written work that follows, completed by the detail of how to produce such different types of work. Research writing has a chapter of its own plus comments to help students avoid racist/sexist language.

Writing essays and assignments and dealing with examinations are the topics covered by Rowntree (1988). The students' attitudes and approaches towards the processes of academic writing are explored through the use of self-test questionnaires. Techniques of handling these different approaches are then well developed throughout the book.

Race (1992) has some useful tips for writing essays and writing up reports. He has several pages of tips regarding exams relating to both revision before and conduct during the examination. Lashley's (1995) approach to essay writing is distinctive in another way by including some practical ideas on planning essays and how to keep to word limits. He also looks at how to write objectively and to deal with the differences of opinion between theorists. Later chapters cover writing up seminar presentations and examination skills.

Four more books that have not been referred to before deal exclusively with the skills of writing. Hall's (1994) 35-page book covers different aspects of writer's block with case histories of 'overcomers'.

The remaining books by Williams cover other facets. Writing essays (Williams, 1995) looks at the planning process and the physical writing of an essay. Williams subsequent 1996 book covers essential writing skills – looking at grammatical rules and the structure of writing. The third book by Williams and Gibbs (1995) is a tutor manual aimed at helping tutorial staff develop students' writing and some guidelines on how to use the other student guides in this 'Oxford Centre for Staff Development' series.

The next feature of academic writing, which is vital in all types of written work, is that of referencing. This is a skill which requires practise and which causes many people, students and tutorial staff alike, to become quite agitated. Looking at the literature being discussed is not altogether helpful as there are differences of emphasis and presentation, factors students cling to.

The key message in all the books is that the student must check the 'house style' of the university or publisher and adhere to, and be consistent in, that style alone. All comments about the efficacy of description could be very subjective so the books are tabulated below (*Table 6.1*) with ways by which students can select the book most appropriate for them.

Table 6.1

Author	Harvard	Van-couver	Other	Brief	Detailed	Secon-dary
Casey		✓		✓		
Cottrell	✓			✓		✓
Cuba and Cocking	✓	✓			✓	
Drew and Bingham	✓	✓		✓		
Gillett	✓				✓	✓
Goodall	✓	✓	✓		✓	
Lashley	✓			✓		
Maslin-Prothero	✓	✓			✓	✓
Murdoch and Davies	✓	✓		✓		
Northedge	✓			✓		
Taylor	✓	✓			✓	✓
Williams	✓		✓		✓	
Young		✓		✓		

The final section of implementing study is, for some students, the most traumatic part of the process — word processing. Many institutions require students to present essays and assignments in a word processed format, and sometimes marks are allocated to this aspect of presentation.

Young (1996) Goodall (1995) Casey (1993) and Northedge (1990) mention word processing and the importance of information technology (IT) but do not develop the subject any further. Taylor

(1992) and Maslin-Prothero (1997) both have a chapter and a variety of aspects related to IT with some helpful, supportive comments for students new to the subject. Further information given can be described as 'tasters' with Maslin-Prothero also giving a list of addresses for information of courses relating to IT for nurses in particular.

After study

Evaluation

When work has been handed in it is normally marked, given comments and a grade, and some type of information is fed back to the student. It is wise for a student to evaluate his/her own work before submitting it, but that bypasses the possibly more objective evaluation of the marker.

Several of the books emphasise the importance of the 'after study' process. Cocker (1987) just discusses how the marks can be aggregated towards a pass and the various permutations of answer types.

Maslin-Prothero (1997) talks about the range of support networks a student can have and this includes tutorial staff. This is also linked with the usefulness of a learning contract before implementation of study. In another chapter she continues with the importance of accepting feedback as a means of personal development and not an opportunity for complaint.

Gillett (1990) and Goodall (1995) and briefly Northedge (1990) make similar approaches but also include feedback from clinical placements. They stress how important it is for students to use feedback to elicit ways of improvement. Cottrell (1999) also looks at how to get 'better' and 'highest' marks. She stresses the importance of tutorial feedback not just the 'mark'. This leads on to encouraging students to review and reflect upon their individual progress – a process useful for developing a personal and professional profile, an aspect of study which is emerging with greater importance. Williams (1995) covers the same ground, pointing out the importance of reflection and using both a learning cycle and peers for development, support and clarification.

Brown (1990) has a different focus relating solely to examinations. This focus is also found in Race (1992) who advises on resit exams and using all the advice offered.

Students who are following all the above processes may also need to write a curriculum vitae (CV) and/or job application forms. For healthcare professionals, portfolio and profile development is very important. Other individuals may wish to write for publication as part of their academic repertoire. Maslin-Prothero's (1997) book covers all the topics mentioned, albeit briefly. Ideas, tips and dos and don'ts are listed. Cottrell (1999) discusses portfolio development and how to turn academic skills into employment skills.

Cuba and Cocking (1994) mention writing a reflective journal and Williams (1995) adds portfolio development as well. Brown and Hawkesley's (1996) book majors on the way an individual's learning style and study skill ability can influence and help create an appropriate personal and professional profile.

Both Goodall (1995) and Gillett (1990) look at writing for publication in some detail. Goodall's book is written with themes identified by the use of icons. For example, within the essay writing section there are icons indicating how the section could be applied to writing for a journal or writing a book. It is worth mentioning that Gillett's book has a series of 'offprints' as appendices which further help to illustrate the subject matter. Young (1996) also includes a brief epilogue on writing for publication whereas Taylor (1992) has a section on copyright.

In his 'ten tips' for format, Race (1992) covers several of the subjects highlighted including how to fill in an application form, how to write a CV and how to prepare for and give a good interview.

Although this section is not exhaustive, it has covered a variety of pertinent subjects relating to studying for different types of university or academic-led assessment. All the texts point out positive aspects for the student to save time and to use the process of this type of assessment for personal growth and development, the acquisition of knowledge and how to 'study in the most effective way'. This information is very advantageous to all students.

The authors suggest that having covered the theoretical assessment that you conduct a literature review yourself on practical assessment. See Walton and Reeves (1999) as a starting point. There is less written on how to succeed in practical assessment.

New message to:

Frantic.Philomena@internetrush.uk

This section is great. I actually read it and it saved me a lot of time. I think it will help you. The authors of this book have done a lot of the work for us — I like that kind of book. However this book has also made me realise that I must do some of the work myself. Don't faint but I am going to follow up on some of the suggested reading that I need.

Charlie

7

Tips on how to get the best from assessment

* Be positive about yourself: be on your own side
* Determine that you are going to work
* Decide how and when you work best
* Find out about and utilise all available resources.

General guidelines

Prepare mentally and physically for assessment

Do not do last minute preparation, ie. the night before

Ensure that you know the guidelines/expectations

Consider specific preparation for each assessment

Make yourself a plan of action: good prior planning will help reduce your stress

Ensure that you are on the right lines. To be sure of this book tutorials

Make sure that you attend or cancel tutorials

When attending tutorials go prepared with the questions you have

Write down the advice you are given

Follow the advice given

Remember **practice is important**, doing something once does not lead to competence. Practise and practise again in a variety of settings, both theory and practice

Ask to do sample questions

Discuss possible answers

Practice under observation/supervision

Help each other – listen to various viewpoints

Link your theory to your practice – utilise research evidence to support your practice.

Use resources

Ask questions when appropriate
Use all forms of assessment to help you build a picture of
    yourself
Recognise potential difficulties and seek advice
If you have dyslexia seek help or support from the appropriate
    department.

Helpful time saving hints

Use a diary – keep it up to date (changes of lectures etc)
Do a schedule
Arrange a study syndicate
Get to the library early with your reading list
Book CD ROM search early
Gather all relevant handouts together
Compile a filing system
Use literature you are given
List useful references/quotes when first reading
Always write your references **in full** so you don't have to repeat
    the search
Sign up for options early
Don't miss deadlines for handing in the work
Know how and where to submit your work
Read the rules relating to extensions of time for work,
        or presenting extenuating circumstances.

In theoretical work specifically:

Check whether you should always write passively, or in the first
    or third person
Acquire and use the **university's guide** to the preferred in- house
    referencing style
Read, read and read before you start writing
Make a plan for written work before you commence writing
Your plan should structure your work
Do stick to the word limit
Refrain from 'waffle'
Make your essays 'marker friendly' – write the introduction that
    leads to a logical presentation

Do a good conclusion bringing together the key points of the essay and making a recommendation or summarising comment

Ensure that you use evidence from other sources of literature to justify a point

Read your university's marking criteria it will help to predict your grade

Make sure that you tackle **each** aspect, and don't miss a vital component.

NB. Appendix should not be longer than 10% of the whole essay

Make sure you do your own work

Specific theoretical assessment

Examinations

Make sure that you have the BASIC information for your examination campaign

Do practice questions

Always make sure that you **read all the questions** carefully

Start with the question you like best but **don't spend too long on it**

Multiple choice questions (MCQs)

Always **read the stem of the question and the four possible answers** before giving an answer

Open book exams

Always take texts that are versatile and have key references in them

Be selective in the books you take in – know them fairly well. If permitted, put 'Post-it'® notes on relevant pages so that you can find things quickly

Do not swamp your exam desk with books

Research Critique

Always **select a topic which interests you** and may be relevant to your practice

Seminars and poster presentations

Do **follow the brief** given to you for the presentation as there is normally a time limit and you should allow for questions to be asked

The time limit is also an indication of the amount of work you should put in

Try to listen to the other presentations

Always **listen to the feedback**

Think about giving your presentation first, so you can enjoy the others

If your assessment involves group work and/or a presentation

Get organised as soon as you know your working group

Swap names and addresses and all means of communication

Set dates for meeting and goals for each

Make sure that visual aids used are big enough for group size

Ensure that the writing is large and clear with key words

If giving verbal feedback of your group's discussion, speak clearly and if possible **stand up, speak up and shut up.**

Practical/practice-led assessment

Be aware of what you might be assessed on

Be involved in the activities that you are going to be assessed on – practise

Ensure that someone observes your performance

Try and get along with your mentor/assessor

Always ask for some guidance on the amount of knowledge that you require

Perform as you should do each day

Be safe always – this might involve recognising your limitations

Get the most out of any practical experience

Be keen – the student who asks, wants to learn

Recognise your areas of insecurity/weaknesses

Be able to justify your actions

Be prepared to adapt to situations.

At the time of assessment

Don't **panic**
Think about the things that you are going to need for the
assessment
Try to forget the assessor is watching you and get on with the job
in hand
Listen to your assessor, welcome their advice, their comments
Show respect and importance towards the assessor's comments
Appreciate the comments, the time and the knowledge they have
tried to impart.

If you have problems with the assessor

Identify the problem in concrete terms: state exactly what was
done or said, the actual fact
Do not let the problem/s go on
Refer problem to appropriate help.

Assessment by peers

Needs to have ground rules
Should not provoke an argument.

Assessment by self

Puts you in the driving seat of your learning
Means you must find out the rules
To be effective it must be planned, negotiated between you and
your assessor, appropriate to the intended outcomes and able
to demonstrate the learning at the correct level.

New message to:

Frantic.Philomena@internetrush.uk
CharlieAvLazy@medullamansions.net

This section should help you both. Even though it's a lot of common sense the points are very relevant and DO help you get through. I am trying to put my knowledge over in this easy, common sense manner so that others, especially patients/clients can understand me. I think this is important because I might think I know it all but it is no good unless I can help others, especially people I will deal with in physiotherapy. See you when we meet in the hols. I intend to ask Pru (if she can make it) about nursing research, especially to do with communication. I think that will help us both. Hope you will join in.

Bertie

References and further reading

Benner P (1984) *From Novice to Expert: Excellence and Power in Clinical Nursing Practice.* Addison Wesley, California

Bloom B (1956) *Taxonomy of Educational Objectives: The classification of educational goals. Handbook one: cognitive domain.* McKay, New York

Brown RA (1995) *Portifolio Development and Profiling for Nurses.* 2nd edn. Quay Books, Mark Allen Publishing Ltd, Salisbury, Wiltshire

Brown M (1990) *How to Study Successfully for Better Exam Results.* Sheldon, London

Brown RA, Hawkesley B (1996) *Learning Skills, Studying Styles and Profiling.* Quay Books, Mark Allen Publishing Ltd, Salisbury, Wiltshire

Casey F (1993) *How to Study: A practical guide.* 2nd edn. Macmillan, Basingstoke

Cocker D (1987) *Successful Exam Technique.* Northcote, Plymouth

Cottrell S (1999) *The Study Skills Handbook.* Macmillan, Basingstoke

Cuba L, Cocking J (1994) *How to Write about the Social Sciences.* Harper Collins, London

Duncalf B (1994) *How to Pass ANY Exam.* Kyle Cathie, London

Drew S, Bingham R (1997) *The Student Skills Guide.* Gower, Aldershot

Edwards SL (1998) Critical thinking and analysis: a model for written assignments. *Br J Nurs* **7**(3): 159–166

Gibbs G (1994) *Learning in Teams – A Student Guide.* Oxford Centre for Staff Development, Oxford

Gillett H (1990) *Study Skills A Guide for Health Care Professionals.* Distance Learning Centre, South Bank Polytechnic, London

Goodall CJ (1995) *A Survivor's Guide to Study Skills and Student Assessments for Health Care Students.* Churchill Livingstone, Edinburgh

Hall C (1994) *Getting Down to Writing: A students' guide to overcoming writer's block.* Peter Francis, Dereham

Hull C, Redfern L (1996) *Profiles and Portfolios, A Guide for Nurses and Midwives.* Macmillan, Basingstoke

Lashley C (1995) *Improving Study Skills: A competence approach.* Cassell, London

Maslin-Prothero S (ed) (1997) *Baillière's Study Skills for Nurses.* Baillière Tindall, London

Maslow A (1971) *The Farther Reaches of Human Nature.* Penguin, Harmondsworth

Murdoch A, Davies B (1994) *An Introduction to Self-Directed Study.* Scutari, London

Nganasurian W (1999) *Accreditation of Prior Learning for Nurses and Midwives.* Quay Books, Mark Allen Publishing Ltd, Salisbury, Wiltshire

Northedge A (1990) *The Good Study Guide.* Open University, Milton Keynes

Peck J, Coyle M (1999) *The Student's Guide to Writing, Grammar, Punctuation and Spelling.* Macmillan, Basingstoke

Quinn F (1995) *The Principles and Practice of Nurse Education.* 3rd edn. Chapman and Hall, London

Race P (1992) *500 Tips for Students.* Blackwell, Oxford

Rowntree D (1988) *Learn How to Study.* Warner, London

Steinaker NW, Bell MR (1979) *The Experimental Taxonomy.* Academic Press, New York

Taylor J (1992) *Study Skills for Nurses.* Chapman and Hall, London

Walton J, Reeves M (1999) *Assessment of Clinical Practice: The why, who, when and how of assessing nursing practice.* Quay Books, Mark Allen Publishing Ltd, Salisbury, Wiltshire

Williams K (1995) *Writing Essays 5: Developing Writing.* Oxford Centre for Staff Development, Oxford

Williams K, Gibbs G (1995) *Writing Essays 6: Tutor Manual.* Oxford Centre for Staff Development, Oxford

Williams K (1996) *Writing Essays 1: Essential Writing Skills.* Oxford Centre for Staff Development, Oxford

Young P (1996) *The Art and Science of Writing.* Chapman and Hall, London

Index